CHRISTY HARDEN

GUIDED
BY YOUR
OWN STARS

Connect with the Inner Voice
and Discover Your Dreams

MAURICE BASSETT

books for athletes of the mind

Guided by Your Own Stars: Connect with the Inner Voice and Discover Your Dreams

Maurice Bassett
P.O. Box 839
Anna Maria, FL 34216-0839

MauriceBassett@gmail.com
www.MauriceBassett.com

Editing by Chris Nelson
Cover art by Chris Molé Design

ISBN-13: 978-1-60025-083-5

Library of Congress Control Number: 2001012345

First Edition

To Kevin, whose faithful friendship, skillful editing, unwavering support, honesty, open heart and impending bottle of Port inspired me all the way through the writing of this book...

To my parents...

And to Dylan, who doesn't need this book at all.

To Love

Contents

Acknowledgements

Thank you... Thank you... Dylan Predko, for teaching me about presence and love by being that, all the time. I love you with all my heart!

Thank you... Kevin Benevedo, for every second of every tireless hour after hour you so generously volunteered, and for those long "five-minute" phone calls that kept me energized and enjoying the process; this is only the beginning.

Thank you... Maurice Bassett, for believing in me and for ushering so much good into the world through your work. Thank you, Chris Nelson, for your meticulous, kind and skilled editing!

Thank you... Laura Miller, Carey Shaw, Mary Haines, Michelle Paisley Reed, and my family (especially my gorgeous nieces), for your thunderous, unquestioning and wildly faithful support. Much love.

Thank you... Amir Zoghi, Ghazaleh Lowe, Jane Thorpe, Jamie Gonzalez and the Los Angeles Oneness Mentoring Group for putting the Truth into words and images that opened my heart and eyes and somehow made everything I'd ever previously "learned" not only click into place, but become real and active in my life. Thank you for giving me a loving space for this journey. Thank you for spreading the Love.

Thank you... Daniel Halem for your queries that prompted me to put fingertips to keys and get this stuff down on paper.

Thank you to the little cadre of Crowtégé peeps who stick with me through thick and thin; you inspire me.

★★★

And to every author of every resource I've referenced here: I've absorbed invaluable instruction on how to rediscover myself and live an authentic life from each of you. Thank you for putting your thoughts and hearts out into the cosmos where I could find them. Many, many thanks do not do your contributions justice.

There's a difference between not *doing* what you love,

and not *knowing* what you love.

Introduction

Does "Living The Life of Your Dreams" Seem Like a Galaxy Far, Far Away?

Introduction

Does "Living The Life of Your Dreams" Seem Like a Galaxy Far, Far Away?

There's a difference between not *doing* what you love, and not *knowing* what you love.

If you fall into the latter category and crave living "the life of your dreams," but when you get right down to it you simply have no idea what that means, *it's because you've lost the connection to your true self and can't hear what your Inner Voice is telling you.*

Are you jamming your GPS signal, blocking your reception and switching off power to your own inner wisdom?

If any of the following statements ring true, I wrote this book for YOU:

- You know you've got what it takes to live your dreams—if only you knew what those dreams were.
- You're unhappy with your life but don't know where or how to start making changes.
- You yearn to live a passionate, purposeful life—but what exactly IS that?
- You're not sure who you are anymore.
- When hearing of a friend or colleague's success, you find yourself feeling jealous.
- You often feel numb and it's hard to make decisions.
- You worry that you're just going through the motions and are missing out on your *real* life.

Sound at all familiar? Now try these on for size: do you

secretly despise statements like the following because you just don't have any clue what they really mean for you and your life?

- Live your dreams
- Follow your bliss
- Listen to your heart
- Be your true self
- Follow your soul's whisper
- Do what you love

If any of this is ringing a bell, you're not alone. I know because that used to be me. Like a lot of people, in many ways the further I got from my childhood, the further I moved into "adult responsibilities" and away from who I really was. By the time I'd reached about twenty-five years old, my "true self," "soul" and "what I loved" were concepts I had very little understanding of or experience with anymore.

Over the years, kazillions of similarly titled books (*Be Yourself!, Live Your Dreams!, Love Your Life!*) accumulated on my bookshelves. I knew I was missing something big and I wanted SO badly to be myself, live my dreams and love my life! But as I continued reading, sooner or later I'd realize I just didn't really know how to do any of that. All the books I read began with the same assumption: that I knew what I wanted to do and just needed some help getting there. But for me, there was a vast chasm of disconnection between myself and a conscious awareness of my true desires. And so, after eagerly devouring the first few chapters of these how-to manuals, my initial excitement invariably soured to a defeated, crumpling discouragement. I began to think maybe there was something wrong with me.

"Wow," I'd admit, "that sounds amazing. But how am I supposed to be 'my true self' and 'follow my bliss and my dreams' if I don't even know what those *are*?"

So I'd buy another book.

Where was the bridge from my out-of-synch life to who I really was and what I really wanted?

I searched long and hard for this elusive but purportedly blissful "true self." I made lists, watched documentaries, listened raptly to anyone who would offer advice, filled out charts, studied graphs, took copious notes and spent a ton of cash on coaches, counseling, seminars, massages and healing therapies. While I definitely benefited from all of this support, I see now that much of it was ultimately unnecessary.

Although it literally took me years (drumroll please), I finally *got* it!

The answer was so simple: I'd been looking *out* instead of *in*. At long last I understood that all I needed to do was *reconnect* with myself, with that someone I'd forgotten I was a long, long time ago. When I finally made this key realization and discovered The Answer I'd been looking for, I thought I'd found the pot of gold at the end of the rainbow. At that moment, I just *knew* that all of my problems were solved.

Ha!

Initially, my profound, "simply reconnect" solution solved precisely nothing. If anything, after that first rush of "getting it" I only felt even *more* at sea. I still didn't know what to do to reconnect with myself to hear my Inner Voice and rediscover the true me. So I searched some more. And then, very gradually, an understanding began to glimmer around the corners of my consciousness—a method to the madness: **The Blueprint.**

The Blueprint I will relay in this book outlines, examines and explains the series of actions I engaged in that eventually evolved into practices which led me to a consistent connection with my Inner Voice and from there into a life that reflects who I truly am, from the inside out. It is this process that I'm about to share with you. But before we start, let's dispel a little bit of mystery by delving deeper into what all of this means at a basic level.

Why Live That "Dream Life" at All??

There's a lot of talk in the media about living a passionate life of your dreams. When it's on network television, all over the Internet and in commercial advertising, you know it's hit the mainstream. But have you ever examined why you'd *want* to live a passionate, purposeful life? Why not just float along with the status quo? A lot of folks do.

While some may truly find contentment simply drifting

through life, I'm going to hazard a guess that you aren't one of them. If you were, you wouldn't have picked up this book.

There's a reason we experience dissatisfaction and angst when we're not living a life that's in alignment with who we are. As human beings, most of us feel a powerful drive to do meaningful work, to make a difference, to help, and to matter.

When we make a commitment to live consciously, to wake up and tune in to ourselves, we start to live lives of passion and compassion. This is healthy not only for ourselves, but for everyone around us and for the entire planet. As human beings, the most vital action we can take is to use this life, this one shot, this incredible gift we've been given, to start where we are with what we've got and do what's in our hearts—following the guidance of that Inner Voice.

And there's your Big Picture answer to the question of why we want to live that "dream life": it's vital to live passionate, purposeful lives because when we do so, we're being who we truly are; our very *best* selves, contributing to the world in unique and meaningful ways.

Oh, and because it feels *fantastic*.

But What IS This Inner Voice I Keep Going on About??

A very good question. If you're going to connect with and follow this Inner Voice, you might want to know exactly what it is and why trusting it is a good idea, right?

Generally, intuition (the Inner Voice) is defined, as it is by Wikipedia here, as "the ability to acquire knowledge without inference and/or the use of reason." For instance, if you listen to it, an alert wariness might warn you to avoid interaction with someone who later displays a dangerous side. Or a feeling of possibility and joy may invite you to sign up for French cooking classes. Both are examples of the Inner Voice.

While we sometimes confuse intuition with unconscious agendas (wishful thinking, for example), the *feeling* of true intuition—the physical and psychological state experienced—is unmistakable. Much more to come on that topic a little later.

Though previously relegated to the status of a "pseudoscience," intuition has more recently been studied scientifically. These studies demonstrate not only that intuition exists, but that some of us rely on this sixth sense more than others do. Professor Marius Usher and fellow researchers at Tel Aviv University's School of Psychological Sciences discovered that intuition was a "powerful and accurate tool." Participants asked to choose between two options based solely on intuition chose correctly 90% of the time.[1]

While defining exactly what the Inner Voice is can actually be somewhat slippery and explanations vary depending on point of view, one thing's for sure: we all have one. Ask yourself: when was the last time you experienced a strong desire to do something but didn't, and it later became one of those, "Man, I *knew* I should've done that" regrets? Or when a sudden thought or flash of brilliance took you by surprise and turned into that scintillating book group, fabulous road trip or fun new hobby? How about that creative burst that kept you up all night putting together an amazing pasta recipe, short story, or presentation?

That's your Inner Voice at work.

Whether you call it your Inner Voice, a hunch, Expanded Self, God, inner guidance, Love, Spirit, gut feeling, intuition, inspiration, conscience, moral code, North Star, God-space or something else, it's the part of you that just *knows*. Our Inner Voice is our best friend, our guide, and our right hand man/woman.

Within this text, I define the Inner Voice as the purest part of us. It is our heart of hearts, the part of us that inhabits our bodies while we're alive and leaves us when we die—the part that doesn't know limitation or untruth. The Inner Voice is the "whole" that is unconditional love. Beyond roles and personas, which are at best only partial expressions of our true selves, the Inner Voice is who we really are.

But can we trust that Voice in our everyday lives? Does it know about taxes and bus schedules and homework? Robert

---

[1] American Friends of Tel Aviv University. "Going with your gut feeling: Intuition alone can guide right choice, study suggests." *ScienceDaily*, 8 Nov. 2012. Web. 31 Dec. 2013.
http://www.sciencedaily.com/releases/2012/11/121108131724.htm
The reference for the original article is: Tsetsos K, Chater N, Usher M. Salience driven value integration explains decision biases and preference reversal. Proc Natl Acad Sci U S A. 2012 Jun 12;109(24):9659-64.

Scheinfeld, in his book *Busting Loose from the Money Game*, says it best when he states, "...unlike a Persona...who might be careless, forgetful, or overwhelmed, your Expanded Self isn't going to take His or Her eye off the ball and starve or ignore your career or personal life. Everything will be just fine." [2]

Our Inner Voice speaks for the big picture and directs us towards people, activities and places that reflect our authentic selves. The Inner Voice is who we truly are underneath all the other stuff.

And what's the "other stuff"? It's a combination and accumulation of mind-habits: expectations, misunderstandings, past experiences, hopes, thoughts, memories, hurts and fears, and is often the filter through which we experience the world around us. The Inner Voice cuts through the "other stuff" like a lighthouse beam slices through fog. It guides us by the brilliant stars of our own sky; our own big picture. We can trust the Inner Voice to know the truth of who we really are. It *is* that truth.

Why Is It so Important to Connect With Our Inner Voice?

Albert Einstein stated that, "The only real valuable thing is intuition." Lao Tzu, ancient Chinese philosopher, noted, "the power of intuitive understanding will protect you from harm until the end of your days." A tad more recently, actor extraordinaire Alan Alda remarked, "At times you have to leave the city of your comfort and go into the wilderness of your intuition. What you'll discover will be wonderful. What you'll discover is yourself."

When we're disconnected from our Inner Voice, we're disconnected from ourselves. Cut off from our intuition, we lose our internal compass and our true North. How can we navigate effectively without inner guidance? How can we possibly live that purposeful, passionate life we long for, the "life of our dreams," if we're disconnected from who we really are? The answer is that we can't; we're lost.

Without the guidance of our inner compass we're at the mercy of guesswork, fears, past experiences and other people's advice—a

---

[2] Scheinfeld, Robert. *Busting Loose From the Money Game.* New Jersey: John Wiley & Sons, 2006.

very dangerous place to be indeed. The past may or may not be an accurate reference point for the present, and as far as others' advice? Not only are others perceiving life through their own filters, but how could they possibly have any idea what lies within *you*, particularly if you *yourself* don't?

Connecting to our Inner Voice is imperative if we want to live our own lives fueled by freedom and purpose. Who is responsible for discovering what that purpose is and freeing ourselves to live by our own code? The answer is staring back at us in the mirror.

The missing link between "lost" and "purposefulness," that bridge I'd been searching for to who I really was and what I wanted, is pure and simple: our connection with ourselves—our Inner Voice. We just have to know how to tune back in.

If you feel disoriented and dissatisfied with your life, the good news is that it's not that you haven't tried hard enough, worked long enough or wanted it badly enough. And it's not too late! You've simply become disconnected from your North Star and lost your way—you can *re*connect; that inner compass is waiting to guide you. You just have to rediscover it and learn to trust it again.

I'll show you how that's done.

Why Do We Disconnect From Ourselves in the First Place?

As babies, we begin life as adorable, dependent little bundles of pure *us*. If you've spent any time with a little one, you know babies and toddlers don't hold back. They don't know or care about hurt feelings, appropriateness, or inconveniencing anyone. They just ARE.

As we mature, we develop a unique and separate sense of self—of who we are and who we're not. Our caretakers and environment begin the process of molding us and we start to learn "the rules." Parents, teachers and influential others hold immense power in shaping our sense of self. We tend to form self-images based on the messages reflected back to us by our caretakers through both their actions and their words.

No matter how we were raised or by whom, the definition of self we arrive at is almost always based on a limited view of who we truly are. Consequently, this view is typically a skewed, partial truth, a misunderstanding of our real selves and what we're capable of doing and being. While our self-concepts are fluid and can certainly change over time, some of us hold on to an early general conclusion that our own Inner Voice isn't all that important, or that it can't be trusted. Whether or not we value our Inner Voice as adults depends heavily on the self-image our caretakers and environment imparted to us as we matured. Were we celebrated, respected and viewed as competent individuals? Were we encouraged or *dis*couraged to trust our intuition and to positively experience independence?

While the degree of trust in our own inner wisdom is typically forged largely by the forces we encounter growing up, there's no denying an X-factor either. Despite upbringing and environment, some folks just roar out of the gate with a screaming inner guidance system and absolutely nothing will derail them. There are countless examples of those who, against all odds, became cracker-jack actors, speed skaters, or animal activists. They just *knew* it from the start and never wavered. Rags to riches stories abound too—people bravely rockin' their own thing no matter what and being richly rewarded for it by the masses. Jay-Z, Oprah and J.K. Rowling come to mind. These are people who at one time or another in their lives experienced periods of crushing poverty and despair. And yet somehow these talented individuals connected strongly with themselves, listened to their Inner Voice and manifested lives of meaningful work and abundance. We all benefit from their commitment to being true to themselves.

Many people whose family of origin left them bereft of any trust in their Inner Voice are later encouraged by mentors to tune in to themselves again. Still others experience unexpected and often traumatic life-changing events that transform their perceptions and allow them to transcend circumstances and realign with their inner wisdom. Our individual stories differ and we may or may not be aware of a specific history that encouraged connection and self-trust or of one that did just the opposite. In any case, there is *another* factor that can interfere with tuning in to our Inner Voice.

The Consumer Connection

Most of us grow up in a culture that, for its own aims, likes to tell us what to do. In an ever-expanding segment of the world's population, culture encourages us to want specific things: a big house, a Lexus, a job with a retirement plan and beachy vacations once a year. It tells us we prefer Coke over Pepsi, or Pepsi over Coke, and assures us we need this watch, that coat, and this eye cream. It reaffirms that yes, just as we suspected, our hair is too frizzy, our car isn't sporty enough and that chunky heel on those boots we're wearing? Ahem, *so* last season.

Pay attention to how many times a day you're barraged with messages implying that what you are or have isn't up to snuff and that you merely need product A, B, or C to fix the "problem." These days, the average person is presented with up to *five thousand* ads per day.[3]

Why? Obviously—the almighty dollar. If you believe you must buy this or that to be acceptable, cool, relevant or worthy, well, the people on the selling end are going to get very, very rich. And indeed, they do! If our wants can be controlled and, even better, transformed into perceived *needs*, then we are willing to spend, spend, spend. So it literally pays to repeatedly whisper in our ears that we're not good enough as we are and that we need to purchase a "solution" (for just twenty-two easy payments of $19.99!). This is the way the modern "American Dream" is sold to us. It's a brilliant plan if no one stops to ask questions like, "Do I really need this?" Or, "What do *I* want? Is this *my* dream?"

If we're not questioning the status quo, we can become discouraged and passive, giving up and just going with the flow. We end up exhausted and barely keeping our heads above water. How can we possibly keep up with everything we're told we should do, be and buy? It's easy to forget that we *choose* how to spend our time and our money; we forget that this is *our* life. We may wake up one day to realize we're living someone else's idea of how life should be and we want to change that.

The problem is that even though we've "woken up" after all of the conditioning and smashing down of our instincts, we often don't know who we are or what it is that we want anymore. Even worse, we don't have the slightest inkling how to find out. So we

---

[3] See, for example: Johnson, Caitlin A. "Cutting Through Advertising Clutter." *CBS Sunday Morning*, 17 Sep 2006. Web. 14 Oct. 2013. http://www.cbsnews.com/news/cutting-through-advertising-clutter/

often just keep doing what we've been doing: going nowhere fast and growing increasingly angry and confused instead of getting back in touch with our Inner Voice, remembering who we really are and living a life that truly reflects *us*.

Time for some good news: no matter how long you've ignored it, stuffed it down or steamrolled over it, your Inner Voice is still there. Underneath it all, your GPS is working just fine and your dream life, your *real* life, is just waiting for you to tune in.

What IS This "Living the Life of My Dreams," Exactly?

Yes, let's get clear on this "dream" thing right off the bat, shall we?

I believe living the life of your dreams means connecting with your Inner Voice and aligning with your authentic self so that you experience life on your own terms. This means living a life completely suited to and directed by you. It's feeling free to be who you really are at all times.

Let go of preconceived notions of what your "dream life" might look like and just get ready to be curious about discovering and rediscovering who you are and what you love. Visions of a huge bank account, a yacht, mansion and endless days spent relaxing under an umbrella on the beach drinking cocktails is what *outside* forces tell us we want. We'll be looking for what *you* want; what *you* love.

By whole-heartedly following the Actions in this book, you will reach the place where you can hear what's "right" and "not right" for you. You will become skilled at understanding what your Inner Voice is saying. If you then choose to act on that knowledge, you'll create an amazing life completely custom-made for you.

Now believe you me, the "choosing to act" part is no cake-walk and isn't *easy* in any sense of the word. But it *is* simple, and if you're willing and persistent, eventually you'll be living from your genuine, authentic self, experiencing life free from self-limitation.

Once you've incorporated all of the Actions within this Blueprint, I encourage you to further support yourself in the journey of creating your dream life by engaging with any of the plethora of books, programs, seminars, coaches and therapists that specifically target putting your dreams into action. But again, you cannot begin taking action on the life of your dreams before you know what those dreams are, and that's why you're here!

In this book, you're going to get better acquainted with the real you and learn to access what it is you truly love. In fact, what we love is actually a portal back to ourselves and thus to the lives of our dreams. And that's what the Blueprint is for—to point you back to *you*, reminding you of who you are. Hello partial, misunderstood you—meet real you! With some time and faithful practicing of the Actions presented here, you'll be on your way. Once you're flying, you can simply use the Actions to reboot when you need them. *Voilà!*

How I Came to Write This Book

If something comes naturally, you don't tend to write a book about it because you don't *think* about it, you just *do* it. If you consider it at all, you simply wonder how it is that others don't just *get it* like you do—after all, it's so simple!

Mastering something that *doesn't* come naturally, on the other hand, takes a lot of time and effort. I wrote about connecting with the Inner Voice because I found myself, years ago, so deeply disconnected that I didn't know which way was up. Over a long period of time and through a lot of hard work, I reconnected and am now living a life I absolutely love and *being* who I really am. I know how to do this stuff and I'm living proof that it can be done, but it certainly didn't come easy for me.

This book, the CliffsNotes version of my journey into connection with my Inner Voice and from there to a life I love, is the distillation of all the work I did to get here. I don't omit anything vital; everything you need is here. Certainly you can take a decade or more, spend a lot of money, gain a lot of "knowledge" and devote a ton of energy to get here as I did; that was my path. But you don't *need* to do any of that. In fact, I'm encouraging you not to reinvent the wheel. When I made it to the other side[4] I

---

[4] By "the other side" I certainly don't mean to imply I've reached some celebratory, graduation-gown end-point. No—what I mean is simply that I'm now living guided by my own stars.

understood that the path is actually quite simple, straightforward, and universal, even though we will each walk it in our own unique style. Let me tell you a little bit more about how I got here.

My Story

Why not start at the point where I'd reached my limit and my life was exploding all around me? Sounds like fun, right?

At about twenty-five years old, I found myself perched uncomfortably on the edge of a purplish tweed chair, staring nervously at a therapist for the first time in my life.

She stared back.

Then came the inevitable inquiry: "Tell me why you're here."

The problem was, I had no answer. Zip. Zero. Flatline. Even as dissatisfied as I was with my life and wanting so badly for things to be different and to feel better, I remember not knowing how to clearly identify what I was experiencing or even how to put my general dissatisfaction into words. I stared at the therapist for several long moments, finally dropping my gaze to the floor, embarrassed. *I should know the answer to this simple question*, I thought, *but I don't.*

I recall finally enumerating several issues I assumed were most likely contributing to my perception that I'd taken some very wrong turns and landed in a very bad place. Suffering from anxiety, frequent migraines, back pain and recurrent respiratory infections, I found myself about to graduate from a master's degree program I generally didn't like and ready to dive into a career I liked even less.

Of course, not *everything* was pitch black for me back then; I was blessed with my wonderful son and close friends and family. But my marriage was rapidly disintegrating and I often felt trapped in my life and deeply dissatisfied with myself. I repeatedly observed myself making panicked, unwise and painful choices that I later regretted. It was as if the weight of years of self-denial and inauthenticity had suddenly hit critical mass. Devoid of a solid foundation of Real Me, my life began to collapse in on itself.

While everyone around me celebrated our upcoming graduation, I slowly imploded. I felt as if I had worked very hard to get somewhere I didn't want to be. I didn't have a clue where to start to understand any of it, let alone make changes. At the same time, it seemed very important to *do* something about all of this.

But what?

I didn't realize then that the root of all my problems was so basic: I'd disconnected from *me*. In a sense, much of my life's situation reflected decisions I'd made without my own approval, without really checking in with myself. Unbelievable as it may sound, I didn't know to do that. At the time I didn't recognize the pervasive dissatisfaction and gnawing confusion as the clarion call of my Inner Voice, weak and weary from years of neglect, still trying to get through.

Why I Disconnected

We each travel our own path, and this one just happened to be mine. If we're connected to our Inner Voice, we've got a clear trail map, but like many people, the connection between the "me" who functioned in the world and my own Inner Voice had dwindled to nothing more than a thread. Thank goodness I still had that!

I don't want to imply that I or anyone else caused my disconnection from myself; that would be inaccurate, as well as neither here nor there. I truly believe that we all make the best decisions we can at each point in our lives with the knowledge, experience and wisdom that we possess at that moment. We're all eventually either on this journey back to ourselves or are working hard at denying the signposts pointing us back into self-connection. You're here, I'm willing to bet, because like I was, you're the former. Because I always find it fascinating to hear how others perceive the ways in which they "lost" and then "found" themselves again, I've decided to relate my own story. Perhaps you'll see yourself or someone you know here.

My parents are both educated, loving and capable people, and like all good parents, mine wanted what they thought was best for me and to protect me from harm. My "sick kid" status made them even more watchful over me. Though my father's parenting style was fairly relaxed and fell a little more on the "let her be a kid" side, my mother was a bit more protective and anxious. Though she has lovingly supported me on my journey, to this day she still bids me goodbye with a tense, "Be careful!"

Due to severe health issues early on, my infancy and childhood were spent in and out of doctors' offices, emergency rooms, and hospitals. Plagued by severe asthma, recurring pneumonia, respiratory infections and collapsed lungs, my first memories are as a baby in a hospital ward, watching shadows shift across the floor through the bars of my crib as the nurses drifted in and out of the room.

Growing up, my fluctuating health defined my life. Sleepovers involved packing medications, relaying emergency information and warding off the ever-present anxiety that I'd begin to wheeze—indicating the onset of an asthma attack away from home, away from the injections my mom administered so that I could breathe. I remember sitting in the backseat of my best friend's parent's car on the way to Disneyland, vigilantly monitoring my lungs; I'd forgotten to pack my inhaler. Dread.

You'd think that growing up like this I'd have developed a keen sense of my body and its ability to relay messages to me, but unfortunately, I did exactly the opposite. Taught to rely heavily on medical intervention, my take-away was that physical symptoms were only indicators of which medication I should take, whether or not I needed to stay home from school, go to the emergency room, get a breathing treatment or endure an injection. In addition, long-term use of Prednisone and other medications often rendered me hyperactive, anxious, sleepy, or otherwise "checked out" to normal internal experiences. I learned with absolute clarity that my body couldn't function on its own and that I needed to rely on others' assistance and on medication for survival. Though that was certainly true for me at the time, you can see how these circumstances may have helped to prime me for a life of self-denial at a relatively young age.

Probably due in part to all of the time I spent sick at home and in the hospital, I did develop a kind of "secret life," reading, writing and pretending, although later on I somehow sadly assumed that this life was just that: pretend.

I recently watched my high school graduation video in which I announced I'd be a writer. A couple of years after graduation, however, I had not yet "succeeded" at publishing anything. I felt as if I'd failed, and at that point I largely abandoned my dream.

Looking back I wonder how I could have expected so much from myself in so little time and with so little experience. Nevertheless, feeling pressure at the time as a young mother to help provide for my family and prove myself "capable," "worthy" and "smart," rather than following my heart, I listened to prevailing opinions of what was "practical" and altered my main course of study. It wasn't just in my career choice, however, that I let others' opinions and "common sense" sway and often completely override my true preferences and real feelings. I discounted or ignored my Inner Voice to a large degree in many other arenas, too. At a fairly early age I was well on my way to a major disconnection.

I look back now with compassion for my younger self and understand the choices I made back then. I'm thankful that I remained true to myself in parenting my son, giving him the authentic, open, loving, goofball mother he deserved; his own authenticity as a human being makes me jump for joy. In other areas of my life, however, I'd clearly begun bargaining, heartbreakingly, with my own soul.

It wasn't until I reached my thirties that I began to truly recognize what was happening. I spent the next decade painstakingly turning the ship around, rediscovering myself and creating a life that reflects who I truly am.

Looking back on my role as a speech pathologist, the irony does not escape me that I worked for many years helping others to communicate, in some cases literally *giving them a voice* while I myself had none. I chuckle, too, when I think about how surprised my younger self would have been to find out that decades later I'd become that writer after all *and* a commercial actor—joyfully inhabiting pretend worlds as I did in my childhood "secret life." I see now that my life has always been a long, slow dance in which I circle, U-turn, and weave this way and that, ultimately spiraling inward toward my true self.

These days I recognize that I'm almost always either consciously or subconsciously teaching myself how to live by noticing "lessons" and examples in the world around me. The *conscious* self-teaching, however, didn't truly begin until the angst and trepidation within my life became so intense that I'd almost completely shut down. Drowning *inside*, I knew only how to reach *outside* of myself for assistance, so I did the only two things I could think of: bought a pile of books and, nervous as hell, sat myself down in that therapist's purplish tweed chair.

Return to Self

My counseling appointment in that chair began a fifteen-year-plus journey of therapy, self-help books, seminars, life-coaching, spiritual seeking and brutal self-honesty. I was so very lost.

My journey back to myself required courage, honesty, stamina and a willingness to do whatever it took to find out what it meant to live a life that felt satisfying and true to *me*. It didn't happen overnight, but little by little, with a lot of teeth gnashing, hair pulling, thrashing around and bumping into walls in the dark, I did finally find my way back. When I arrived, a relieved and joyous ME blurted out, "Welcome home! We're going to have such an amazing life!" And boy, has *that* been the truth.

The fact that I had no idea I'd stepped *off* of a path (what path??) of hearing and listening to myself, let alone experiencing the power of my own Inner Voice, made for a very long journey back. It doesn't have to be that way for you.

Instead of following a clearly marked trail like the one I outline in this book, I meandered along, picking up a bit of insight here, making a little leap over there, and running headlong into a quagmire of quicksand in between. I didn't own a map, I didn't have a plan, and I didn't possess any big-picture understanding. For many years, I often felt blindfolded, blindsided and wildly confused. I didn't know where I was going, what I was going *for* or what I was missing. I just knew that there was more, and that sinking backwards into where I'd been was no longer an option.

Though I rarely moved forward with anything resembling grace, I'm forever grateful that somehow, I just kept going. Every new insight was like a fresh breeze, and with each tiny epiphany I breathed more freely. The aha moments kept coming and I forged ahead, gradually stripping away the things that separated me from my true self and thus from a life I loved.

Now, as I pursue the subtleties of this art we call Life in happy anticipation that I still have much to experience, I live my days on my own terms, continually challenging perceived limitations and creating a life experience that I can only describe as Magical—with a capital M.

Though I'm certain I'll continue to deepen my experience of living in true authenticity over the course of my lifetime, my actions and decisions now overwhelmingly flow from my true self. Do I experience ups and downs? You bet—I continually find pockets of resistance and work through them. Do I ever disconnect and find myself struggling? Sure, that's part of our human experience; such is life—it's a process. I'm well aware, for instance, that in times of duress I'm particularly susceptible to blocking out my intuition and slipping into a familiar pit of confusion—it's a well-worn detour for me. But that happens less and less often over time, and here's the important thing: I now know how to *re*connect and find my way back, literally in an instant.

As I discover and rediscover who I am on deeper and deeper levels, I now see my life as an adventure and understand that joy emanates from the acknowledgement of our oneness with our true selves, each other, and everything around us. While I'm fairly certain that we never actually arrive at an "I made it!" destination in our lives, if we're willing to accept what's there, follow our hearts and step into the unknown despite our fears, we can certainly experience more and more freedom, joy and connection on our journeys. To me, *that's* truly living, and I'm enjoying every bit of it.

Once you remember how to reconnect with your true self, *then* you can go out and live this marvelous "life of your dreams" you've heard so much about—but not until then. Not until you've tuned in to your Inner Voice and mapped the stars that make up the constellations in your own personal sky.

This book contains the Blueprint that shows you exactly how to do that. Within these pages I've condensed the key concepts, experiences and practices that allowed me to reconnect with my true self and live a life guided by my Inner Voice.

Though every day isn't always jazz hands, twinkly lights, unicorns and kittens, I'm most definitely *home*. Reconnecting with my Inner Voice gave me my life back. With this book I hope to give you a jump-start on your own journey to reconnect with your inner self and create a life *you* love.

Within these pages you will discover eight Actions that will transform your life, if you let them.

My advice?

Let them. Decide right now that you'll be honest enough, kind enough, open enough, patient enough and brave enough to find out who you really are and why you're here.

What's the alternative?

The How

How to Use This Book:
Getting Our Bearings

The How

How to Use This Book: Getting Our Bearings

We often hear that our answers are inside of us. True! Your Inner Voice is with you all the time, trying to get through. But if you're starting out, like I was, in a place of almost complete disconnection from that Inner Voice, you don't know *how* to get to wherever that place is inside you to find the answers—or even what questions to ask to get started.

If you have little or no experience listening to or trusting your intuition, you pretty much *have* to start outside yourself. But all that's required is for someone to show you how to open the door to your inner self and turn up the volume of your internal guidance system. And then? With practice, you'll take it from there. You'll live by your own compass, and you'll rely on your own Inner GPS. You *can* get to the inside and you *can* find that place of self-wisdom. This book will show you how.

Along the way you will come to understand why your signal gets jammed in the first place. As this becomes apparent, you will clear a path for your Inner Voice to come through and then learn to build strength and trust in that Voice. Allow me to save you years of blindly searching around and show you how to accomplish this much, much faster than I did.

What I'm setting out for you in this book is a method with which you can hasten your journey to an understanding of who you are underneath everything else—at the core of your heart, or the heart of your core.

I'll show you how to reconnect, to turn up the volume and tune in to your own personal radio station.

Within these pages you will find the Blueprint; a set of hierarchical Actions designed to amp up the volume of your "still small voice." Hearing that Inner Voice loudly and clearly—and *respecting* it—will direct you to what you love, and from there onto the path leading to the life of your dreams, because you'll finally know what those dreams *are*.

As I'll note throughout this book, this process is simple, but not necessarily easy.

I've organized the material presented here into steps designed to allow access to your inner wisdom as quickly as possible. But this isn't like fast food, where "quick" is synonymous with "unhealthy." Quite the opposite. "Quick" here means I've cut out what you don't need and included only the highest quality and most salient information to expedite your journey. I'm not dictating a recipe to you for the life of your dreams; that's what your own Inner Voice will provide. I'm simply showing you how to clear your pantry of all of the unhealthy stuff you've been consuming that's clogging your system and blocking your Inner Voice. Like a clean diet, the information in this book will allow you to free yourself of extraneous junk, discover the true you, and begin to function on a much healthier level.

But Doesn't This Take a Lot of Work??

Well, yes, and no. In a way, the transformational practices contained within these pages are the *opposite* of work, as we're concentrating on removing obstacles and allowing you to be just as you are. You'll get to the real you, sans the extra goop that's taking up space and obscuring your true self. You will relearn how to listen to yourself. This takes patience, kindness, perseverance and commitment, and certainly isn't easy, but it isn't "work" in the traditional sense.

Your role here is to read the material with an open mind. Come at it with a willingness to try something new and step outside your comfort zone as you follow the Actions contained herein.

Does it Matter that My Life is Different From Yours?

Not at all. This book is not a map to get to a specific *place;* it is a map to get you to *your* map. Only *your* map will lead you to where your treasure chest (your real-you life) is buried. Your treasure will be unique, and all your own.

Let's be clear. This book is about one thing: getting out of your own way so that you may uncover, discover or rediscover your Inner Voice. Your Inner Voice is your own personal guide. It will chart a course to the most amazing life you can imagine.

The Actions I lay out are not "secrets." I didn't invent them, and you can find them individually in various forms in any number of places. Unless otherwise stated, however, the interpretation of each concept within this book is filtered through my own individual analytical style, my life and my experiences, and is undeniably (for better or worse) my own.

The Actions within these pages are clearly numbered, explicated, and laid out in an easy-to-apply Blueprint. They will show you, step by step, how to cultivate a life in which you gain consistent access to your Inner Voice, discover what it is you love, and thus experience the opportunity to live a life that floats your boat beyond all your expectations, just as they've done for me.

Your results are all about your commitment to yourself; the power of these Actions is in their consistent and sincere application. Your arrival here at this moment in your life is a game-changer—if you allow it to be.

Before You Begin, Ask Yourself: "How Important Is This to Me?"

How important is it for you to begin to hear your Inner Voice, to be guided by your own higher knowing to a life that will have you smiling when you wake up in the morning, energized and happy to start your day?

If you're yelling "Woo-hoo! SO important! Bring it on!" then you'll welcome the practices I've prescribed here.

We all experience days when we're incredibly inspired and life is fun and easy. On the flipside are those days when we'd rather crawl under a rock than out of bed. That's to be expected. What's important is that as you move forward with the Actions, keep putting one foot in front of the other and stay focused on the Blueprint—no matter which side of the bed you wake up on.

And don't worry: this isn't a one-shot opportunity. If for some reason you aren't able to complete the Actions in one fluid sequence, simply continue to practice what you've learned so far and jump back in, implementing new Actions when you're able. This is about you discovering you, on your own time.

Do, however, work toward implementing these practices consistently. That's where the strength of the Blueprint lies.

What we will be accomplishing in these Actions is a clearing of space—a cleanse or life-detox of sorts—while also adding a few simple practices to your day. I promise they will not take up much time and that ultimately you'll find that, rather than feeling burdensome, these Actions will *open up* time and mental space for you. You'll likely begin to look forward to them and experience feeling more and more energized. You'll start to notice more joy and lightness and begin to have *fun*.

YES, FUN!

A Word or Two About Health

This is not a diet or exercise book. However, the correspondence between physical health and feeling good in general is undeniable. Feeling good means more joy, or at least easier access to it. In my own life, I delved into various options for eating and exercising until I found a combination that worked well for me. I'm healthier now than I've ever been in my entire life.

For me, I found that as I began to eat unprocessed, whole, raw, vegan foods, I started to feel better and better. My asthma, brain fog, respiratory infections, migraines and lower back pain gradually faded almost entirely away. Today I take no prescription medications and, with the exception of a few trips to the dermatologist and chiropractor to keep things shipshape, haven't needed to visit the doctor in years. With *my* health history, that's saying something.

While I certainly don't recommend any one plan for everyone regarding eating or exercising, I encourage you to explore healthy options for yourself. Get enough sleep, eat real food, and move your body. The healthier you are, the better you'll feel. People who feel good deal with fewer distractions, including physical aches and pains and diminished energy, and ultimately stand on a strong foundation for growth and happiness.

We all start where we are, and wherever *you* are is just fine. Just give your diet, sleep habits and exercise regime a once-over and keep in mind that if you address any related issues either prior to or during your time with me here, you'll be optimally positioned for clarity and progress. You may find that the more connected to yourself you become, the more motivated you'll be to implement healthy habits!

Resources

Along with my own experiences, I've included some resources I discovered during my own journey. I simply provide them for your perusal. They are not "required reading" but merely sources of information that may assist you on your journey. Some may appeal to you now, others may not sound interesting at all, and some you may wish to revisit at a later time. As with all resources, I encourage you to take from them what makes sense to you and leave the rest. This is how I approach any resource myself. Benefitting fully from this Blueprint does not require that you read, watch or listen to anything I suggest in the *Resources* sections at the end of each chapter; it's merely bonus material. If you follow the Actions with an open mind, remain willing to step into unfamiliar territory and approach this process with bravery, authenticity and a willingness to follow your heart, you will get to where you need to be: you will find your map and connect with your inner wisdom.

Expansions and Guerilla Actions

At the end of each Action you will find *Expansion* and *Guerilla* sections. These sections are optional, and provide additional opportunities to deepen your engagement with the Blueprint. *Expansions* propose activities to expand your experience of the Action, while *Guerilla* sections suggest more time-intensive and/or integrative activities to more completely incorporate the Action's influence into your daily life.

Partners

Some people prefer to read and learn alone; they find it easier to concentrate. Others enjoy working with a partner. If you've got a supportive best friend or companion to work through this Blueprint with, two is often more fun than one! A book club can be even *more* fun, and is actually an ideal setting for sharing experiences while learning concepts, processing ideas and completing the Actions. It can also provide support for you and others along the way. At the end of the book you'll find a few suggestions to get you started if a group experience sounds like fun. A little hand-holding and cheerleading can be a beautiful thing!

However you choose to experience this book is fantastic—even if you change plans midstream. Find what works best for you.

I suggest completing the Actions in order, one per week, which will allow ample time to cement each one before moving on.

If you need more time on a specific Action, take it, but be careful not to get bogged down. Keep moving. Consider all of the Actions together as your Blueprint for connecting with your Inner Voice and aligning yourself with a life you love. The Actions build on each other, and you'll continue to practice the previous Actions as you proceed with the Blueprint, so you'll be able to delve deeper and deeper into each Action at your own pace throughout the book and beyond. Integrating these practices into your life will continually keep you tuned in to yourself and guided by your Inner Voice.

It's time now to buckle up and enjoy the ride! Aaaaand....

HERE WE GO!

Materials

Dig up or purchase the following:

- Regular sized notebook (spiral is fine) with pockets inside the covers—lots of pages is a must!
- Mini notebook to keep in your pocket or purse
- Three or four pieces of poster board or card stock (to hang up—go as big as you'd like)
- Daily calendar (if you already have one, by all means continue to use it, or use the one provided on most cell phones)
- Timer
- Post-it notes (to use as tabs)
- Pen or pencil you enjoy writing with
- Reminder items—you can gather these as you get to the Actions that require them. They will be items you already own that will serve to remind you to practice the Actions during the day.

Along the way I'll suggest a few optional materials you might enjoy. You can acquire these when the time comes.

I encourage you, throughout the book, to put your own stamp on everything you do here. Get fancy and fun with the materials if you want to, but it's certainly not required. You'll use your notebooks to record everything you do in this Blueprint, and combined with a few additional projects we'll put together, they'll serve as your "Guide to You" and keep you tuned in once you've completed the Actions. We'll call our notebooks the "IV Notebook" and "Mini IV Notebook." IV stands for Inner Voice, and the information you collect within its pages will be like nutrient-rich intravenous fluid to keep you hydrated, healthy and on track.

Bon Voyage!

The Who, What, Where and When

The Actions

Action One

Weathering the Inner Storm:
Inviting Calm

Action One

Weathering the Inner Storm: Inviting Calm

Before we locate our North Star or even lift our gaze skyward, we must first find calm amid the storms that rage within us.

For the Inner Voice to become consistently audible, we need to first quiet the noise that drowns it out. A good portion of that noise emanates from *within* us. Finding calm amidst that chaos is our focus for this Action.

As human beings, part of what makes us unique is our particular make and model of brain. Infinitely useful in navigating our lives, our brain's functions range from regulating our breathing to understanding quantum physics. One of the brain's main jobs, of course, is *thinking*, and wow, is it ever good at *that! So* good that it keeps plugging away, day and night, whether we want it to or not. We've all experienced the pressing desire to sleep, and yet ye olde brain spins on and on, keeping us awake long past our bedtimes. Often our thoughts appear unbidden, circulating as unnecessarily detailed, useless replays of the past or forays of fantasy into the imagined future.

Vexing!

From this familiar background of mind-chatter arises the age-old desire to silence this thinking for a bit—to stop the yammering. But *can* we ever do this?

Well, yes and no. As Eckhart Tolle suggests, expecting a brain to stop thinking completely is as unrealistic as expecting a heart to stop beating. It's just doing its job—and thank goodness for that! But there *is* something we *can* do: slow down our internal dialogue and *remove our focus from the thoughts*. Revolutionary! Not by banishing thoughts, but simply by placing our attention elsewhere we can free ourselves from our own crazy-making heads! It's actually possible to let our thoughts run in the background like an old movie we've seen seventeen times while we relax and drift off to sleep (or do anything else, for that matter). Disconnecting and dis-identifying from the chatter helps us rest and experience calm, for sure, but it also allows us to clear a quiet space within ourselves where we can become aware of the Voice of our own inner wisdom.

Aha! *Now* we're getting somewhere.

So how do we remove focus from thought and start to experience some peace? Some seek inner calm through elaborate ritual while others prefer zoning out in front of the TV. Many of us rest our minds listening to music, participating in a sport, creating art or caring for another. Although the choices are endless, most activities employed to attain a calm internal state are really just variations on a few themes: distraction, detachment, engagement, and present-moment awareness.

Labeling any of these methods as "good" or "bad" is erroneous; most may be used in either destructive or beneficial ways. However, as mind-calming techniques are often enacted unconsciously—that is, we engage in them without knowing we're doing so—they frequently go unanalyzed. My rule of thumb? Using any method to avoid the pain of a situation that needs to be addressed becomes destructive. Employing a method to experience one's life in a more conscious, authentic and healthy manner, on the other hand, is beneficial.

Our Method

For our purposes here, we will be finding calm within present-moment awareness. What do I mean by "present-moment awareness"? It is, as the name implies, a state of *presence*—an integrated awareness of both our internal state (including thoughts, feelings, physical sensations and reactions) and our external environment, without a particular attachment to either. Present-moment awareness is a centered focus in which we notice what is within and around us without becoming caught up in thinking about those observations. In this state of calm alertness we enjoy the clearest access to our Inner Voice as well as to our memories and analytical abilities, resulting in ideal conditions for determining accurate and appropriate action.

Present-moment awareness allows us to place our full attention on life as it is happening *in the moment*, which is the only place life actually occurs. When our awareness is focused on the constant chatter in our heads (commentary, predicting the future and reviewing the past), we lose our ability to "be in the moment" and to actually experience our lives as they unfold. Detaching internal focus from (and identification with) constant repetitive and circuitous thought is imperative in the quest to clarify our internal experience and allow the Inner Voice to come through loudly and clearly.

While other methods of calming the mind involve busying it with activities or detaching from ourselves to avoid thought or emotion, present-moment awareness neither denies nor pushes away our experience but rather accepts it. This allowing enables conscious awareness of our thoughts and emotional patterns as well as our identification with them, which eventually affords us freedom from unnecessary automated internal reactions that keep us repeating old patterns, shatter our clarity and distract from the Inner Voice.

If we spend the majority of our lives inhabiting the present moment while judiciously employing thought for analysis, recalling, planning and executing actions as needed, then we are consciously living our lives. And that, my friend, is where we want to be!

The Clarity of the Present Moment

One summer when I was about twelve, I visited my best friend who'd recently moved away. Prior to her moving we'd spent pretty much every waking moment together and I missed her like crazy. Visiting her was an incredibly special time for me. I remember so many tiny details about that visit with crystal clarity: her mother preparing bacon for breakfast, my purple blossom-flecked PJ's, shopping with my friend for striped bikinis, our tanned legs as we posed for pictures with her little black dog. I particularly recall a moment just after waking up one morning: I lay cozily in bed as the sun shone on the carpet next to my bed, illuminating specks of dust drifting in the warm air. My friend slept peacefully across the room and no one else was awake yet. I remember wanting to hold on to that moment forever, so I concentrated as hard as I could on everything I saw and felt. To this day I can vividly recall that moment like I'm right back there in my friend's sunny bedroom.

Later in life, I realized that my general lack of awareness of the present moment allowed much of my life experience to slide by me unrecorded and, in many instances, unnoticed. The kind of heightened awareness I experienced when I visited my friend that summer is the kind of awareness we can exist in every single day.

The best and most effective practice I'm aware of for training ourselves to tune into the present moment is... drumroll... *meditation.*

WAIT! STOP!

If you're feeling any resistance to the term "meditation" or have previously endured painful, negative experiences with this practice, hold up! Banish all lilac-hued, flower-child, peace-signed, hemp-clothed, hippy-dippy associations and read on. All I'm talking about here is sitting silently for twenty minutes (and we'll work up to that), calming the mind by removing identification with and focus from inner chatter and working with emotions that inevitably arise. Period. No bells and whistles here. We're just being still, accepting who and where we are right now, and focusing on this experience of being alive in the present moment. This practice clears a path to allow us access to our deeper wisdom.

Meditation has no religious connotation here. It is a simple activity that benefits all of us, not just those who came of age in the 1960's. The point is to practice observing our thoughts and emotions and realize that *they are not us.* Who we truly are is an awareness apart from our thoughts and emotions. If the term "meditation" bothers you too acutely, just call it "quiet time" and move on.

Certainly many individuals hold widely differing beliefs about how to go about the practice of quiet sitting. No matter. At its core, meditation is a very basic concept which simply allows us relief from identification with thoughts and emotions, and that's all we need here.

My own experience with meditation spans a number of years and various practices. I've found each incarnation worthwhile, and currently I combine several techniques that work well for me. I also vary the method depending on my physical, psychological and emotional state at the time, but my main focus is always simply to relax and focus my awareness on the present moment. Many times, I do nothing but relax my entire body and focus my awareness on that feeling of relaxation, which brings me back into the here and now. If I could employ only one of the Actions in this book, it would most definitely be this one.

HERE WE GO

We'll be incorporating present-moment awareness into our daily lives by engaging in the following two-part exercise:

1. Relaxation
2. Quiet sitting

Relaxation allows the body to release tension, which in turn facilitates ready engagement with the quiet sitting exercise. As noted, "quiet sitting" merely refers to the practice of sitting still for a period of time and focusing attention on the present moment. Day by day, both practices increase the awareness of who we are apart from our minds and assist in the sloughing off of accumulated stress and physical tension, which aggravate mind chatter and suck up energy that is best spent elsewhere.

As far as I'm concerned, there are basically two types of meditation. The first simply focuses on the present moment with the purpose of observing our inner lives and ultimately removing focus from and identification with thought and emotion. The second may incorporate visualizations, music and/or guided recordings to obtain specific results, such as weight loss or reduction in anxiety. In the morning we will be employing the first method. In the evening, although we aren't aiming for self-improvement in the traditional sense, you will have the option of incorporating music, visualization and any additional supports you'd like to include.

In this Action, we will practice meditation two times daily in twenty-minute sessions, once soon after waking and once before bed. Why twenty minutes? Most studies reveal significant health and wellness benefits derived from meditation practiced in twice-daily sessions of twenty minutes each. These many benefits include lowered blood pressure, a need for less sleep at night, and boosts in feelings of well-being. Longer meditation periods are fantastic; I just want to make sure you're getting these basic benefits by practicing at least twice daily for twenty minutes.

You may notice that sometimes it takes fifteen to twenty minutes just to really let the tension go from your body and for you to experience a separation between yourself (as the observing awareness) and your thoughts. That's fine, although I will often extend my own quiet sitting time just to be in that restful state of existing for a longer period. You, of course are welcome to do the same.

Morning Meditation

Materials

- Quiet spot
- Your IV Notebook
- Writing utensil
- Timer
- Mat or small pillow to sit on (optional—you may also simply use a chair, a towel, or the floor)

Time

Twenty minutes, two times a day. We'll work up to this over a period of four days.

➢ Day One: Using the steps below, sit quietly for five minutes.
➢ Day Two: Sit quietly for ten minutes.
➢ Day Three: Sit quietly for fifteen minutes.

➢ Day Four: Sit quietly for twenty minutes. We'll stay here for the rest of the Blueprint. If you feel like sitting longer on some days, do it. It will only benefit you. But don't burn yourself out. Unless you're really on fire, let yourself be satisfied with the twenty minutes and move on. You're good.

HOW

Here are the steps you'll follow each day:

1. Choose a quiet spot. Select a location in your home where you won't be disturbed and to which you can return twice daily without interruption. Turn off your phone ringer and do whatever else you need to do so that when you're in your spot, you'll be able to focus on the task at hand. Have a timer or clock available.

2. Pull out your IV Notebook and dedicate a section (using a divider tab) to "Meditation" (or "Quiet Space" or "Josh's Spa Time" or "Amanda's Me Minutes" or whatever you come up with—put your own spin on it if you'd like). Record the date and time of your meditation. Briefly jot down how you feel pre-session and then again post-session (for example: "2/24, 10:00 a.m. Pre: a little grouchy. Post: calmer, more grounded"). Keep the notebook open and close to you.

3. Grab a snack! Some say it's best to meditate on an empty stomach, but I prefer having at least a little something in my belly before I begin, otherwise I find myself distracted by hunger and a growling gut.

4. For the morning meditation, it's preferable to sit up if possible. Either sit in a chair with your hands turned palms up on your thighs, or if it doesn't hurt your back, try sitting cross-legged on the floor in the traditional "lotus" style. I do this with a small cushion under my rump, and find this to be the most comfortable position for me. You may use any pose that allows you to relax while maintaining your position and staying awake and aware simultaneously. If you're in physical pain when you

sit, use a recliner or support your back with pillows, for example. Do what works. You may keep your eyes open, or close them during meditation. I tend to close my eyes initially, to tune in and relax, and sometimes open them later on when I'm focusing a gentle attention on both my surroundings and inner experience.

5. When you're ready to sit quietly, set your timer for the appropriate number of minutes. If you're watching a clock, note when your time period will be up. Initially, even five minutes may actually feel like a long time, believe it or not. That's ok. Just do it. This is *you* time, and it is very important. You need this. Quiet space is imperative and foundational for reconnecting with ourselves. Some find it helpful to do a bit of yoga or some stretching exercises prior to quiet sitting. Feel free to ready yourself in any way you find supportive, and then begin. Here's how it goes: **sit**, **relax**, **breathe**, and **focus**. Easier said than done, so let me break it down:

-   **Sit**: Sit however you're going to sit, and close your eyes.
-   **Relax**: Stretch your arms, your neck and whatever else needs stretching, then settle in. Let all of the tension in your body go. If you have to scratch an itch during quiet sitting, do it, but make an effort to move as little as possible during this time. Take six very deep diaphragmatic breaths (tummy expands, filling with air, and then breathe deeply into the chest before exhaling) in through your nose and out through the mouth. Picture breathing in pure energy and exhaling any tightness or stress. Let all tension go by tensing and releasing each muscle group from head to toe in order, top to bottom, if this is helpful. Next, again beginning at the top of your head and proceeding to your toes, imagine a wave moving through your body that melts away any remaining tension. Throughout your session, check in with your body whenever it occurs to you, releasing any tension that may return.
-   **Breathe**: After the first six deep breaths, breathe normally.
-   **Focus**: Place your attention on the bottoms of your feet. See if you can feel the energy in them—a tingly, buzzy or

pulsating sensation. As soon as you feel that, move up to your entire foot. Feel the energy there and continue experiencing that sensation one body part at a time until you reach the top of your head. You will feel a kind of aliveness throughout your entire body, a presence to the energy within you. Attuning to this awareness will become automatic with practice, and when that happens you won't need to start at the bottoms of your feet—you'll just be able to place your attention on the energy within your body.[5]

Continue to focus your attention as described above for the allotted amount of time. Alternatively, you may focus on your breathing. During your sitting time, return your focus to your feet or to your breath as soon as you become aware that your attention has drifted.

Night Meditation

Materials and Time

Identical to morning meditation.

HOW

Night meditation may take any of several forms; simply select whichever version appeals most to you depending on your needs at the time. You may also choose to repeat the morning meditation in every way or vary it by changing your physical position. For example, you may lay down flat on your back, arms at your sides with palms facing upwards, or with one hand over your heart and one slightly above your stomach. If you'd prefer, you may lounge in a comfortable chair. Just make sure you stay relatively still in a comfortable position for the prescribed period of time. As noted, we'll mirror the morning meditation time allotments by working up to the full twenty minutes. Once you get the hang of it, feel free to engage with the night meditation for as long as you like; if

---

[5] I learned this particular method from Amir Zoghi and Ghazaleh Lowe (see *Resources* for more information); Eckhart Tolle and others offer similar exercises.

you're using a recorded meditation, for example, there's no need to stop in the middle if it lasts longer than twenty minutes. Do the six breaths and the relaxing wave, and then check in with your body's energy.

You may choose from any number of meditation options, such as:

- A downloaded meditation, guided visualization, or relaxation recording on your computer (you'll find many free programs on the web).
- A favorite relaxing, instrumental CD or other recording.
- A meditation app (also available for free—you can pay for one if you'd like, but the important thing is to use one that you find relaxing).

Over time you can build up a library of different options to choose from. Or, you may simply repeat the morning meditation—it's up to you.

Resist the urge to review your day during sitting time. Do this before you start the timer if you'd like, and then let it go if possible (if not, simply allow it to be there but don't focus your attention on it—keep your attention focused on your feet or breath). The basic idea is identical to the morning meditation: relax, release tension, acknowledge and allow whatever is going on in your head and body to exist there without it sucking up your entire attention.

For both morning and evening meditations, don't be too rigid about this process, but at the same time make sure you DO it. Take it down to the most basic level if you'd like: sit or lie down in whichever position is most comfortable and focus on your body energy or breath for the suggested number of minutes.

Common Issues with Meditation

★★★

The Pressure to be Calm

When you start meditating it is inevitable that as your brain zips you away from the present to the past or future and in and out of emotions, the thought, "Shoot! I'm supposed to be CALM!" will enter your mind. But let me be clear: meditation is about observing emotions and patterns of thought and understanding we are an awareness underneath them. Eventually we see that we can simply acknowledge thoughts and emotions, experiencing and releasing them without engaging in the drama they usually incite. The end result is a calm awareness that's conducive to everything amazing, including connecting with our Inner Voice. The "goal" of meditation here, however, if we can call it that, is not to "be calm" per se, but to simply allow what's there to exist in our minds, while realizing that we are the presence beneath the thoughts and emotions. Calmness is actually the *result* of finding a patient, kind willingness to be with whatever is within us, not an action to be taken in itself.

Boredom

I remember when I began meditating I thought, "Oh geez, how boring! What am I going to be doing if I'm not THINKING?" We're so conditioned to intellectual activity and busyness that for some it's hard to imagine just sitting still without also experiencing boredom. We're far more used to distractions. Hardly a minute goes by without input from some source: the television blaring at us, the radio, the Internet, *Facebook* and *Twitter*, most of which are available 24/7.

Sometimes I catch myself scrolling through *Facebook* on my computer while responding to texts on my phone, listening to a podcast and checking email all at the same time. Good grief! For many of us it's usually not so much that we're distracting ourselves intentionally, it's just that we can become somewhat addicted to this feeling of "busy"—a feeling which masquerades as productivity and provides us with a false sense of meaning or purpose. This busyness, however, disconnects us from our bodies, the present moment and, of course, from the Inner Voice.

We need to do a bit of a re-boot here and remember that peace and calm not only occur while sitting by a lake on vacation or when we've checked off that ever-elusive last item on the to-do list. Peace is our birthright; it is our natural internal state when we remove focus from the chatter (inside and out—more on "out" in the next Action) and bring our attention back into our bodies and into what is happening in the present moment. Peace is what allows us to regulate emotionally, to go to sleep at night without prescription drugs and to connect with our inner wisdom. If we cultivate a relationship with and a respect for quiet, we reconnect with ourselves and integrate our minds and bodies, providing a space for our true selves—our Inner Voice—to come through.

Here's a little secret: the "emptiness" that we uncover when we cease all the internal and external yammering is not *empty* as we understand empty; it's actually a sense of fullness we experience as *joy*.

Sleepiness

Sleepiness during meditation tends to be an issue for everyone sooner or later. If you *do* fall asleep when you sit down to meditate, allow it, if you have the time. Most likely your body is running on a sleep deficit and simply needs more rest. If possible, continue with your meditation as soon as you wake up and attempt to address your sleep-schedule issues ASAP.

If you've gotten plenty of sleep and still find yourself nodding off, it's most likely because you're not focused on the present moment. Bring your attention into the energy in your feet or to your breath and see if that helps.

One technique you can try for increasing alertness is to simply notice and watch the sleepiness in a focused, present way. This tends to dissipate the tiredness. Alternately, you may find that doing a few jumping jacks or other simple exercise prior to sitting down may increase your alertness during sitting.

If sleepiness persists in the absence of any identifiable cause, consider the role that falling asleep may play for you. Is it possible it serves a function, such as allowing you to avoid unpleasant thoughts or emotions you'd rather not experience that might surface during meditation? If this or another underlying purpose is a possibility, remind yourself that whatever comes up during meditation is part of the process and that you'll be okay.

Thoughts About Thoughts

As I mentioned in the introduction, one of the main reasons to meditate is to remove focus from (and identification with) the endless chatter of thoughts in our brains. So what do we do with the thoughts that come to us while meditating?

The answer is this: Nothing. Let them be. This might sound easier said than done (and initially it is), but it's quite possible to simply notice and acknowledge the thoughts and then release your focus from them, bringing your attention back to your body energy or to your breath. While thoughts will continue to arise, our intent is to let them move through our minds and not get "stuck" on them. Quiet sitting time is BEing time. The thoughts are welcome; there is no negative emotion or judgment attached to their appearance, continual reappearance or content. We simply acknowledge them, wave them on and return our focus to body energy or breath. I sometimes find it very effective to simply say to myself, "Here," when I find myself following a distracting thought. This is a reminder to let the thought go its own way and return my focus to the present moment. I also sometimes visualize placing a particularly persistent thought in a shoebox, labeling it, and stowing it on a shelf to pull down for review after my sitting session.

Previously I also suggested keeping your IV Notebook open and close by. Occasionally during meditation, an idea that feels important enough to write down will enter your consciousness. If this happens, go ahead and do it. Then you can leave the thought on the paper and let go of it in your mind. Only do this if absolutely necessary, however, and guard against letting your meditation time morph into a brainstorming session.

While the vast majority of thoughts that flash through your mind will be repetitive, unimportant chatter, you'll also notice that as soon as you give it a little space and quiet, your mind will occasionally remind you of vital tasks you've forgotten or may spontaneously offer solutions to problems you've anguished over for weeks. Record these inspirations, but *only* these, in your notebook so they don't disappear into the mist. Do not think about them once you've jotted them down; you can deal with them after your sitting session.

In meditation, you'll start to recognize that the same thoughts and emotions tend to surface over and over again, and that there are only a few major themes. My own thoughts revolve around the following: planning, judging myself or others, fantasizing, contemplating, repeating bits of random phrases heard previously, narration, and problem solving. Oh, and singing. My brain does a *lot* of singing! Eventually, allowing, acknowledging, experiencing, accepting and releasing the thoughts will become a bit more like second nature, and they won't grab your attention or pull you away from your focus as easily. Your mind will tend to slip into a calm state more and more quickly and easily during your sitting meditation and later, in your active life as well.

Emotions

Emotions often flare up during meditation. This is normal, and a welcome part of the process. The emotions that arise are the same for all of us: versions of either love or fear. They may either directly follow a thought or seem to appear out of nowhere. At some point, emotions that you *really* don't want to deal with will surface for you during meditation, just as they do outside of meditation. That's actually a good thing, even though it might not feel like it at the time. Each arising emotion is a chance to clear some of its energy from your system. Resisting experiencing these emotions will simply cause them to hang around longer; they're there for a reason and need to be felt. Ever heard the saying, "what we resist persists"? That's what I'm talking about here. Most of us aren't used to doing anything with strong emotions beyond using every trick in the book to *avoid* feeling them.

Like all other living beings, we innately seek pleasure and avoid pain. While most of us don't think twice about experiencing "positive" emotions, we usually resist the "negative" ones with all our might. When it comes to painful emotions, however, we've got to experience and move through them; otherwise they persist in a nasty cycle that can continue for an entire lifetime: feel pain, run, feel pain, run, feel pain, run.

That pain is still there because you haven't yet allowed yourself to experience it! Only after being experienced can it move out of your system. While I know that in a way it seems counterintuitive, believe me—actually feeling those strong emotions will dissipate their power and begin to free you from their grasp. Meditation provides us with a safe place to experience emotions so that we can identify and accept them and move on.

I've experienced meditation sessions in which I laughed, cried and became suddenly angry all in a matter of twenty minutes—and that's not unusual or unique to me! It's normal, healthy, and okay. Experiencing emotions during meditation is part of the process, and it means you're genuinely engaging with the practice. While at first it may feel unnatural or even scary to simply sit there and experience the internal uproar, it's not harmful. In fact, if you actually concentrate on the physical sensations that accompany a "negative" emotion—such as, "my stomach is tight," "my chest is burning," or "I want to run away"—without resisting, the power of the emotion will begin to dissipate over time, sometimes within a matter of moments. Don't analyze. Let it come and go. Here's how:

Working with Emotions in Meditation: The Acceptance Process

The following steps outline a simple process to apply when emotions arise during your sitting sessions. I credit Amir Zoghi[6] with introducing me to these instructions, which he refers to as the Acceptance Process.

Step 1. Notice and acknowledge the emotion. Stop running. You don't have to label what it is you're experiencing, but if you can and want to, go ahead. For me, labeling sometimes helps me identify the emotion when it resurfaces somewhere else ("Oh, this

---

[6] Zoghi, Amir. "The Wisdom, Truth & Freedom Experience."
See: http://amirzoghi.com/programs/the-wtf-experience/

is that old insecurity thing again") and allows it to release more quickly. But labels are only labels, and the important thing is to simply acknowledge the emotion.

Step 2. Turn to face the emotion. Sit with it—which means FEEL it. *Really* feel it. Allow it to be there. Don't try to manipulate it, make it go away, or change it. Don't try to feel better. Just give it space to exist as it is. Dive into it. Watch it. If it feels like it's going to drown or suffocate you or make you go crazy, that's okay. Let it feel however it feels and don't resist it. You won't actually drown, suffocate or go crazy. This is how we move through the emotion—it can't actually harm you. Just let yourself fully experience whatever is there.

Step 3. Notice *you* are not the emotion. Just breathe.

Step 4. Sit and allow the emotion to be there until you notice it simply isn't present anymore. It will dissipate, sometimes surprisingly quickly.

Repeat steps 1-4 when emotions resurface. As you accept what you're experiencing, each time you re-experience an emotion, the "charge" that accompanies it will lessen until the emotion, or at least your attachment, identification and engagement with it, simply dissipates completely. This may take one session of accepting the emotion, or for deeper, more entrenched emotions, it may take many sessions over a long period of time.

It doesn't matter where the emotion comes from, although you may experience sparks of understanding around its inception or persistence during this process, which may be helpful in the release of the emotional charges. The key to moving through the emotion and releasing its charge is simply allowing it to be there and experiencing it, no matter how many times it arises. This is old pain that needs to be released. When the emotion is processed, it may still arise as a ghost of itself; the difference will be that it will hold no power over you any more as its charge will have faded away. Sticking with this practice, you'll start to find that you're able to work with whatever's there inside of you—you don't have to fear it anymore, because you don't have to actually "handle," "manage" or "control" the stuff that you didn't want to feel; you can just BE with it, and it's okay. At some point, emotions and memories stop being the enemy.

Making a commitment to yourself to experience your emotions during meditation instead of pushing them aside and distracting yourself from them will deepen your meditation and begin to clear some of the emotional reactions that often unconsciously inform your behavior. Meditation allows us a private space, our own personal workshop, where we can work with any areas of resistance, slough off excess gunk and free up more and more space for our true selves to come through. I find that whatever I do in meditation seems to magnify its application outside of meditation as well, enriching my experience in countless ways.

One Rule

There's just one hard and fast rule here: you are not allowed to have any judgment about your "performance." Meditation is *not* a performance! It is what it is: you cultivating an acceptance and an awareness of being right where you are. Some days will be easy, others will seem like a struggle. It's okay. All of it is just as it should be. If you find you're beating up on yourself or judging in any way, as soon as you notice it, accept that it's happening and place your attention on your body energy or breath. As Pema Chödrön points out in her incredible little book, *When Things Fall Apart*, if you are present with paying attention to your breath for only ten seconds out of the entire meditation session, then that's what happened. No big deal. She says:

> You just find time each day, and you sit down with yourself. You come back to that breath, over and over, through boredom, through edginess, fear and well-being. This perseverance and repetition—when done with honesty, a light touch, humor and kindness—is its own reward.[7]

This is simply a practice, not life or death. You will never be asked to compare your experience with an "ideal," there is no goal line, and you are not expected to be anything other than exactly

---

[7] Chödrön, Pema. *When Things Fall Apart: Heart Advice for Difficult Times*. Halifax: Shambhala, 2002.

who and where you are right now. Simply being exactly where you are is the point. You'll start to notice over time that just being present becomes more and more natural, because with practice we start to learn how to stop resisting and to be patient with ourselves; this is key to reconnecting with the Inner Voice. While I'll provide you with more Actions to assist in tuning in to yourself, you'll be miles ahead if you can understand the critical importance of how powerful the ongoing process of releasing resistance to "what is" can be.

In a nutshell, there is no "pass" or "fail" here. Meditation is an end in itself. You've succeeded if you've spent your allotted minutes practicing placing your attention on the present moment, observing and allowing your internal state, waving thoughts on and experiencing any emotions that arise. It doesn't matter how "well" you did this. If you did it, good job—gold star!

Don't worry about anything, including whether or not you're doing it "correctly." Just follow the instructions as best you can and make the time to sit quietly for these few minutes twice a day. Expect that it may take a little while for you to let go and stop struggling—or rather to accept the struggle and redirect your attention to the present moment. Stick with it and I predict that you'll find meditation time to be one of your very favorite periods of the day. Over time you will learn a lot about yourself through this practice; it will lay bare the inner workings of your mind and heart.

Expansion

If you'd like, decorate your quiet spot and make it cozy and comfy, adding items that invite calm. You might set aside a special set of soft clothes to wear to get you in the mood, for example, or perhaps set up a calming ritual to complete beforehand: tea, a bath, listening to calming music, lighting candles, or reading a passage from a relevant text. Whatever feels relaxing to you is terrific. A small heater or special blanket in the winter or a fan in the summer might also be nice. If you have a picture or item that reminds you of the importance of being able to connect to your inner wisdom, place it in your meditation space.

Guerrilla Meditation

When you get really great at focusing on your body's energy or your breath, you might start to practice what I like to call Guerrilla Meditation. Guerrilla Meditation is the ability to experience a meditative state of presence exactly where you are, at any time: riding the bus, sitting in a doctor's waiting room, or coloring with your eight-year-old nephew. Simply practice tuning in to your body's energy or your breath whenever you think to do so, wherever you are. This ability to return to the calm state of present moment awareness in almost any situation will come with practice.

Resources

Resources rich with additional information and knowledge regarding relaxation and meditation abound. In addition to just Googling the heck out of it, here are some of my favorites:

Books

Guide to Stress Reduction by L. John Mason, Ph.D.
When Things Fall Apart: Heart Advice for Difficult Times by Pema
    Chödrön
A New Earth by Eckhart Tolle

Music

You'll find many relaxing music CDs available for purchase even in chain stores such as Target or, of course, online, not to mention the multitude of recordings you can access from the web for free. Make sure the music serves simply as background and that you don't get mentally caught up in it in any way. When I was playing in bands, for instance, listening to music during meditation was a frustrating distraction as I kept neurotically counting beats. Thankfully, I don't do this anymore, but the point is to only use music if it's not a distraction for you.

Online

If you're interested in the Acceptance Process I described or are curious in general about my references to Amir Zoghi or Ghazaleh Lowe, check out the following:

- academyofintuition.com
- befreepeople.com

I've found their teachings immensely helpful in all areas.

Pre-recorded meditations

Glenn Harrold offers several relaxation and self-improvement apps. I have also used Steve G. Jones' recordings on CD and online at stevegjones.com.

Action Two

Gazing Skyward: Stop the Madness and Tame Your Life

Action Two

Gazing Skyward: Stop the Madness and Tame Your Life

To locate our center, our North Star, we must not only find calm amid the inner storm—we must also tame the outer chaos of our lives so that we may extend our gaze beyond our noses and look skyward.

In Action One we began to clear some internal space, allowing ourselves some breathing room and creating a calmer atmosphere in which our own personal GPS could be distinguished above the inner chaos. For Action Two we'll be freeing up some more space in *external* portions of our lives by eliminating unnecessary action and creating calm in our schedules.

Ever look around and notice the laundry pile is suddenly a mile high, mold has once again claimed the shower for its own and you've forgotten your sister's birthday? How about suddenly finding yourself sharing the car with empty water bottles, several overflowing mystery bags, and something that smells vaguely like rotting fish? Feel like you've been rushing around without a moment to spare for the last, um, lifetime??

Yep, I felt like that a lot, too. I'd respond by spending a day or two cleaning everything up. That felt amazing... for a few days or so until the cycle started all over again.

What I lacked was a simple but efficient system for achieving both inner and outer order. When I'm disconnected from myself, life left unchecked becomes more and more hectic and disorganized. The second law of thermodynamics is often interpreted to imply that all systems tend toward disorder, and wow, do I find *that* to be true!

The more we tune in to our Inner Voice, the more outer order will simply appear to happen on its own. When we're tuned in, we just suddenly feel inspired to do the dishes, vacuum or finally sit down with the taxes. But until we get there, let's buy ourselves some space and time by putting an easy system into place that assists us in organizing our days.

Survival Mode

Most of us live very busy lives, often perceiving that we must simply try to get through our days in "survival mode." That is, we feel we don't have enough time to get everything done—certainly not with any degree of real quality—so we rush, multitask and compromise quality simply to make it through to the end of the day. The problem with this? Oh, where to start?!

Let's take it a chunk at a time.

First of all, this core "survival mode" concept that says we need to just get through the day is *false*. It's a victim-y mental construct that's gotta go—STAT! Many folks—and I've been there myself—fight through their days, discouraged and disheartened, feeling constantly stressed out, believing they're buffeted about by circumstances beyond their control. The problem is that they often fail to examine this belief—and it *is* simply a belief.

When we buy into the paradigm that we have no control over our experience, when we're flailing around, reacting to one stressor after another like we're playing a game of Whac-A-Mole, we hand over our power and live day to day in what feels like a barely conscious and confusing fight just to stay afloat. This way of being can become a habit.

But we don't have to live like that—we have a choice. We alone decide how to structure our days. We are always in charge of how we deal with events *internally*; that is, in how we *respond* to what happens externally. We all have the power to live consciously in a way that doesn't result in stress and hurrying, and instead provides us with a sense of calm and joy. When we realize this, we can begin to tackle the detrimental coping behaviors we engage in to respond to the "chaos" of life, namely:

Rushing

Rushing is a result of forgetting that we have control over how we spend our time and thus how we experience our lives. Hurrying confiscates our feelings of lightness, spaciousness and freedom and makes everything feel like a race—stressful! I'm not going to go into what happens to our brains and bodies under prolonged stress; most people are well aware that it's not a healthy state to be in. Rushing also breeds forgotten lunches, keys locked inside cars, and oh-my-goodness-how-embarrassing-I'm-wearing-two-different-colored-socks kinds of days.

In short, when we're rushing we're constantly focused on the next thing—getting to work, the project waiting for us at the office, getting the kids off to school—instead of the present moment and what's right in front of us. I can't tell you how many times I've driven somewhere and, upon arrival, couldn't tell you how I got there. Have you ever screeched to a halt at the end of your day and wondered what the heck you actually *did* for the last ten hours?

Any time our focus is on the past or future instead of on the present moment we lose our feelings of calm and joy, along with the ability to consciously and mindfully live our lives—because we've lost our connection with ourselves.

Multitasking

Remember when multitasking was all the rage? The glorious rush of false efficiency as you answered a phone call, wrote a check, clicked around online, organized your desk and updated the calendar all at the same time? Although social forces and modern expectations still encourage multitasking, we now know, via oft-repeated scientific studies, that the brain's ability to actively focus is limited to attending to one or two items at a time. Earl Miller, professor of neuroscience at MIT, explains that "people can't multitask very well, and when people say they can, they're deluding themselves. The brain is very good at deluding itself."[8] He notes that what really happens when we multitask is that our attention rapidly shifts from one item to the next. This activity-hopping burns extra minutes and results in mistakes—and less-than-stellar overall work quality. Researchers are also recently finding that when we multitask, we actually begin to *lose the ability* to focus on one thing for an extended period of time, and that our creativity takes a big hit as well.[9]

Another consequence—one not mentioned by Dr. Miller but which won't come as any surprise to anyone who has read thus far—is that multitasking also results in an *inability to stay connected to the Inner Voice*. When we're attempting to attend to three or four or five things at once, maybe making breakfast, emailing, dressing the kids, getting ready for work and conversing with a spouse all at the same time, it's almost impossible to also attend to the present and to how we're feeling—to our inner guide.

Compromising Quality

Compromising quality occurs when we perceive that we "don't have the time" to do it right. I'm talking here about the big picture as well as the details. Sure, there are detaily things we don't really care about quality-wise, like pumping gas or washing dishes, where we might argue that paying attention and going for quality isn't all that important. But I beg to differ.

If our intent is to reconnect with ourselves, we would do well to accomplish everything as mindfully as possible. Doing so affords us a sense of calm and joy in almost any everyday activity—from making tea to heading up a board meeting. By eliminating unnecessary tasks, consciously choosing our activities and completing them with presence and focus, it really is possible

---

[8] Hamilton, Jon. "Think You're Multitasking? Think Again." *NPR*, 2 Oct 2008. Web. 15 Oct 2013.
http://www.npr.org/templates/story/story.php?storyId=95256794.
[9] Intagliata, Christopher. Producer. "Science Friday Podcast: The Myth of Multitasking." *Science Friday,* 10 May 2013. Web. 17 Dec 2013.
http://www.sciencefriday.com/segment/05/10/2013/the-myth-of-multitasking.html

to experience every action as a practice in awareness. Awareness happens only in the *now*, which is also where we connect with our Inner Voice. If we compromise quality in the little things, the big picture (made up, as we well know, of the little things) suffers as well.

Though continual mindfulness takes a lot of practice, there's no hurry to reach any "level" of competence with this skill. It's helpful to realize that this calm observing presence is actually our natural state of being; it's there underneath all the busyness and upset that's distracting us. Rather than *adding* something to our to-do list, reconnecting with mindfulness only requires *releasing* our focus on the distractions. Simply beginning to notice when we lose our connection with the present moment will suffice to increase our awareness over time if we keep at it. This increased awareness is vital, as each moment we reconnect with that awareness and allow ourselves to drop back into the present is a moment we reconnect with our true selves.

Practicing Mindfulness

Now that we're clear on how non-awesome survival mode, rushing, multitasking and compromising quality are and how they actually block access to our inner wisdom, let's stop the madness and take a breath.

Ahhhhhhhhhhhh.

There. Now:

Imagine a life in which you experience awareness and calm throughout your day, no matter what you're doing.

Picture cultivating mindfulness, lightness and care in everyday activities, such as placing a ten-dollar bill in your wallet, greeting a good friend or watering your plants. Feel the texture of the bill on your fingertips, notice the golden flecks in your friend's hazel eyes and the silvery water droplets as they form on the leaves.

Can't you feel the sense of calm already? It's a big, clear, open feeling—*it's connection to ourselves.* When we're aware of each moment, those moments open up and present us with a pulsating vitality. It is within this awareness of the moment-by-moment rolling out of our lives, like film unspooling from a movie projector, that we get to experience what it means to truly be alive.

It takes practice, but not only *can* you cultivate this keen presence, it is *essential* that you do so if you want to reconnect with your Inner GPS.

But How Do I Do That??

Easily. And I'm not kidding! Like every Action in this Blueprint, this one requires an openness to doing things a little bit differently than you may be used to and a commitment to yourself to apply the practice, but it won't, by any means, be beyond your capacity. Consistent application of this Action will return your investment in spades. You'll find that incorporating the practices below will quickly imbue you with a relaxing sense of calm and automatically encourage connection with your true self.

In addition to encouraging an awareness of when we've lost focus on the present moment, Action Two focuses on three interlocking practices that will support a return to mindfulness:

1. Prioritizing activities.
2. Leaving enough time for the activities we've prioritized.
3. Performing only one activity at a time.

First let's look at these individually, and then we'll see how we put them to use.

Practice One: Prioritizing Activities

At a very basic level, our most important task as human beings is to decide how we will spend our time each day. This is a mandatory assignment, whether we consciously allot our time and energy to activities or let chaos, lack of focus, others' agendas and procrastination take the wheel.

Before I understood the importance of prioritizing, I used to find myself frazzled, hungry, tired and down in the dumps much of the time. Disconnected from myself and not in a state of presence, I simply followed the path of least resistance all day long.

Here's how a typical day went for me:

Since I didn't structure my days, I rarely got to bed in time to get enough sleep before work the next morning. I'd set the alarm to wake up at the last possible moment. I couldn't very well arrive at work naked, so getting dressed and making myself presentable trumped eating breakfast and packing a lunch. Off I'd go, hungry, tired and already dragging. By lunchtime I was starving, grouchy and often headachy, but having packed no lunch I usually grabbed a snack at what I'd erroneously categorized as a "healthy" fast food place, ultimately only accelerating my declining energy and rapidly deteriorating mental state.

Because I didn't structure or prioritize my time at work efficiently either, I'd frequently toil away far beyond quitting time, something I often felt frustrated and angry about. Then, as I had usually put off grocery shopping, I'd sometimes get fast food again for dinner. By the time I arrived home, it was too late to go to the gym, and since I felt like I'd had no "me" time at all, I'd stay up late. The next morning, the cycle started over again. I felt haggard and behind the eight ball. Like a lot of people I knew, I lived for the weekends, when I tried to catch up with the sea of responsibilities I'd "had no time for" during the week—a Sisyphean task.

That was many years ago, and while I can't imagine living like that now, I certainly know many people who still do. If I'm describing your life here, have hope! Action Two is just what the doctor ordered.

While there's nothing wrong with unstructured time, when we find ourselves spending it on activities we don't care about while neglecting to prioritize what *is* important to us or what we really need, it's time to examine how we're going about our days. If you're still part of the rat race, spinning around on your little wire wheel feeling exhausted, powerless and angry, know that you don't have to do that anymore. If you're ready to start looking at things a little differently and reclaim your life, you've got the right book in your hands.

Let's get something straight: I'm not a fan of planning every second of every day. I'm actually a big fan of a little using-of-the-brain for logistics and a ton of spontaneous inspirational jaunts and fun—as much of that as possible! The truth is that by implementing a little structure and eliminating the chaos, you can actually open up much more time for yourself. The more you tune in to your Inner Voice, the more you'll find you're able to select activities you enjoy while leaving space for spontaneity. What I'm suggesting for this current Action is that we *choose* our activities instead of letting habit, obligation or apathy dictate them to us—and then we enjoy the heck out of them, or at least complete them on time with the attention they deserve. We need to decide what's really important to accomplish and what's not, which requires not only honesty with ourselves, but a new practice of consistently thinking *quality over quantity*. This brings us to the next interlocking practice.

Practice Two: Leaving Enough Time

This one is quite simple. Once you've decided on some activities you'll accomplish for the day, *leave enough time to do them.* So if you're going to a movie, this means factoring in the time it takes to drive to the theater (allowing for traffic), parking your car, walking from the parking lot to the movie theater, purchasing your ticket, buying snacks if you'd like, and getting to your seat. Making sure you leave enough time requires only a few seconds of planning and will save you from arriving late, feeling rushed, flustered, frustrated and stressed. Novel concept: leaving enough time allows you to enjoy not only the movie, but the entire experience of anticipation and arrival.

Remember, when planning an activity, take the *entire activity* into consideration. We have a tendency to mentally shorten the actual time we think of as "the activity" and omit necessary related tasks. For instance, in the past when I thought about juicing in the morning, I'd mentally include the time required to feed the veggies through the machine but would *not* allocate any time for getting the food out of the fridge and washing it before I put it through the juicer. Nor would I plan for cleaning the juicer afterwards. Though neither task required more than a couple of minutes, not mentally including them as part of the task of "juicing" consistently had me running a few minutes late in the mornings. By including (and completing) *all* the actions necessary in a task when we plan to do it, we avoid unnecessary rushing and frustration—not to mention the depressing sight of a sink full of juicer parts when we get home!

Practice Three: Performing One Activity at a Time

This practice is also uncomplicated and straightforward, but it may take a bit of discipline on your part, especially if you're used to multitasking around the clock. Here's the simple rule: when you're doing something, *do only that*. Period. Resist the urge to simultaneously watch TV, text, or plan tomorrow's schedule. If you're eating dinner, for example, focus your attention on the taste and texture of your food, on how the fork feels in your hand, how green the lettuce is and how the candlelight reflects off of your knife (Yes, candles! Why not!?). If you're eating with a partner, focus on him or her; really *be there*.

One. Thing. At. A. Time.

Schedules and Routines

I used to despise the concepts of "schedule" and "routine." I craved freedom from demands on my time and didn't want any on-paper reminders or rigid plans messing with that freedom.

But schedule or no schedule, the truth was that I craved freedom precisely because I didn't have any. And why not? Primarily because I was disconnected from myself and the present moment and thus wasn't consciously choosing how I spent my time; I had no understanding of the three practices described above.

I got a twinkling of understanding one day when a therapist suggested the following: instead of drawing up something I labeled a "schedule" or a "routine," I could merely create a list of activities I wanted to "make time" for. Somehow this took the pressure off; *this* I could handle! I started to understand how prioritizing my activities could actually usher in the sense of freedom I wasn't yet experiencing in my life.

Currently, I do enjoy a flexible and loosely structured repeating sequence of daily events (okay yes, a routine) that evolved organically as I consistently made time to do what was important to me on a daily basis—things like getting enough sleep, meditating, walking my dogs, writing, drinking fresh green juice and enjoying free time. Since my schedule is dictated by my Inner Voice, nowadays "routine" is a word with far greater *positive* connotations for me. It's what keeps me feeling good, connected to myself and doing the things I love. Rather than dictating my time and stealing my independence, my routine *opens up* time and creates a sense of freedom in my days. The general sequence of my day flows beautifully, and when I purposefully deviate from it— maybe while traveling or when I just want a different kind of day—that's perfect. I know I can return to it whenever I want to.

The Unexpected

Do all days go as hoped and planned? Please. Of course not! But that's okay. Life is not about planning every second and rigidly carrying out those plans; life is about experiencing what it is to be alive—which happens to frequently include a lot of spontaneous, unexpected stuff. As they say, expect the unexpected!

What we're doing in Action Two is providing a bit of structure to decrease stress, hurry and mind-spinning, but also to give you some space for inspiration, spontaneity, and the unexpected— along with room for your Inner Voice to come through! If you consistently and consciously set out your activities, most days you'll experience a sense of calm and the pleasure of time well spent, with room for the unplanned.

Know that scheduling is only a tool, and that changing what you've planned when you feel like it is not only A-OK, but actually very important, particularly as we move further into the Actions.

While most of the time your new loose schedule will go off without a hitch, other days, of course, the baby will spit up on your blouse right before you're about to leave the house, a gust of wind will fling your presentation papers all over the street on your way to a meeting, or a dog will need rescuing, causing you to miss a much-anticipated date. *C'est la vie!*

If you decide to go with the new activities (changing the blouse, retrieving your papers or rescuing the dog—always rescue that dog!), take them in stride, reframe what your day looks like and regroup. No one said the first plan was the *right* one! Part of true freedom is realizing that our lives unfold in a field of unlimited possibilities—not just the ones we plan for! Carry on and accomplish whatever you're doing with awareness—one thing at a time. Resist the temptation to throw up your hands and grumble, "To hell with it! I'm picking up two cheeseburgers and watching Netflix for the rest of the day."

But: If you do choose the burgers and movie every once in a while, simply write off your entire day-plan and roll with it— what's the big deal? It's *your* life and I'll bet you that in a day or two, no one, including you, will remember or care!

The key here is to experience going in a new direction as a *choice* instead of a knee-jerk reaction to what you perceive as a series of chaotic events taking over your life and ruining your plans. *Bend like the willow.*

Being True to Your Word

As Danielle LaPorte (one of my very favorite motivational divas) suggests in one of her videos, "Do what you say you're going to do." Of course sometimes stuff comes up and we need to postpone, reschedule or cancel, but knowing our intention is to follow through on our commitments encourages four powerful results:

1. Activities and tasks you really don't want to do get filtered out. If you find yourself saying "yes" or "maybe" to unwelcome invitations or requests just to buy yourself some time, knowing you'll cancel later, *stop*. It's messy and unnecessary. Buy yourself even *more* time by being honest and brave enough to just say, "No, but thanks for offering me this opportunity." Of course, if you really *do* need to think about it, state that. Remember the saying: "People will respect your *no* if they know they can count on your *yes*."

2. You might start to become more comfortable with social situations. If you're someone (like I was) who halfway dreaded social interactions because you were used to constantly agreeing to things that you really didn't want to do, when you start being willing to just say "no," you're free to enjoy social contact without the fear of getting "cornered" into anything.

3. Resentments all but disappear. When you stop doing things you don't want to do anymore, you realize that it wasn't *others* taking advantage or controlling you. It was simply *you* not taking ownership of and responsibility for your time.

4. And perhaps most importantly: you start to absolutely trust your OWN word and stick to the commitments you make to *yourself*. This is ultra important to the Inner Voice, believe you me.

HERE WE GO

Using the three little interlocking practices of *prioritizing, leaving enough time* and *performing only one activity at a time,* we're going to open up your sense of time. We'll be adding some light and flexible structure to your day, which will magically rescue you from rushing, multitasking and compromising quality. This in turn will allow space for calm, joy, and your Inner Voice to come through.

Materials

-   Your IV Notebook
-   Writing utensil
-   Calendar

Time

A few minutes, twice a day; once in the morning and again in the evening. A couple of minutes just after meditation in the morning and just before your session in the evening are perfect. That way you start your day off consciously and wrap it up in the same way.

HOW

1. Using your calendar in the traditional way, simply note activities to be completed on the appropriate days. This keeps you from missing appointments and having to remember

everything in your head—exhausting. You'll be referring to your calendar each day when completing the rest of this Action.

2. Now designate a substantial section of your IV Notebook for "My Time" (or create a more fun-o-rific title if you'd like). If you're using a spacious calendar that includes a daily section with hours of the day printed out, you can use that instead. Or, if you'd like to use a separate notebook for this, feel free—if you're using your notebook instead of your calendar, you'll eventually need another notebook anyway as you use the space you've allocated for "My Time" in the IV Notebook. It isn't critical at this point, however.

3. Each morning following meditation, draw a vertical line down the middle of a new page. On the left side of the line, make a list of what you'd like to make time for that day. Make sure to check your calendar and include any appointments or other events you've already scheduled on that date. Even if your list consists of one item, such as "relax," that's great. We're building a habit here.

4. Now review that list. Is there anything on it that really isn't important or necessary? Cross it out and/or write it on your calendar to complete on another day. Remember that while using this Blueprint you're learning to give yourself some space to tune in to the inner you, so cut out any activities that aren't vital. Think quality over quantity—and I mean it—from now on.

5. Star items you really want to accomplish. Limit these to three or at most, four items.

6. Now, on the right side of the same page, write out the hours of the day (unless of course you're using a calendar with preprinted hours). Fill in your important planned activities into the hour slots. *Leave enough time.* As discussed, also jot down driving/walking times and prep activities, such as showering or packing a snack (you won't always need to do this—pretty soon you'll begin to more accurately assess task times on your

own without thinking through every little step). Don't forget to include your meditation time!

Ultimately this process should take you no longer than a couple of minutes, although when you're first beginning, take a few moments more to make sure you've got the important stuff in there. This gets faster and more automatic by the day. NOTE: The space between the activities you've outlined is for you to relax and/or do whatever you feel like doing in that moment. What a concept!

7. Go about your day. Keep your attention focused on each task at hand as much as possible (as previously mentioned, this will take practice so be patient with yourself) and enjoy the sense of space and calm. Notice how there is actually an underlying joy that begins to glow through your day when you complete tasks with care and focus. Crossing off each task as you go isn't necessary, but it can be fun. Make sure that the starred items are completed if at all possible, even if you do none of the other items on your page.

8. At night, just prior to meditation, review your notebook (or calendar) page for the day and transfer any incomplete tasks to the next page for tomorrow (repeat drawing a vertical line down the middle of the page for the next day), or write them in your calendar for a different date if that's appropriate. Remember to star important items. If additional activities occur to you that you'd like to write down on the calendar or on tomorrow's list, do that. Reflect on how focusing your attention on the *now* seems to expand each moment. Then enjoy the feeling of satisfaction from a day consciously lived!

As you go about your day, remember that when unexpected events arise, engaging with them or not is often up to you. While "no" can be a difficult word to say and may carry with it consequences you'd prefer to avoid, when the boss asks you to come in on the weekend or a friend just *has* to talk with you *right now,* remember that in the vast majority of situations you'll encounter, no one can manipulate, overwork or take advantage of you without your cooperation. In fact, those terms are merely intentions you've ascribed to someone else's actions (correctly or incorrectly, it doesn't matter). In essence, someone has simply made a request/demand, which you will either choose to comply with or not. Just realizing that you're *making a choice* immediately reclaims your power from the situation, taking you from "victim" to "empowered." Pretty cool, actually!

Some unchosen and non-preferred events, however, will periodically arise in which you truly don't have a choice regarding whether or not you'll engage with the situation, such as getting rear-ended. You'll just have to deal with these when they appear. That's fine. Try reminding yourself when things don't unfold the way you'd planned: "Well, this isn't what I'd prefer, but that's okay. It's what *is*." But even then, having a greater sense of calm and efficiency in your day will help you deal with those unexpected events all the better. Consider these two related points: First, while we typically *believe* we know what's best for us, in reality we often don't have a clue, later finding ourselves grateful for events that at the time seemed like the *last* thing we wanted to have happen. Second, we can only plan for what we know, thus rendering it impossible to foresee events that often wildly exceed our expectations and blow our small-minded plans out of the water.

You'll find that Action One and Action Two jigsaw together in a symbiotic relationship in which each benefits the other, allowing both to be accomplished more easily. Actually, all of the Actions work together like that, which we'll see as we go along.

Expansion

If it flips your pancake, go all-out with a separate, designer notebook (or decorate your own) for this activity. Maybe get ahold of some fun stickers and go to town on this Action! I often find that new paper products motivate me beyond all reason.

Guerrilla Calm and Organization

Some people are just naturally organized and neat. The rest of us can benefit from taking a look at what we've collected in our lives and then prioritizing what we love and use and want to keep, and what can be shed. It's amazing how much mental and emotional weight certain items can carry with them, such as a photo that reminds you of a difficult divorce each time you pass it or a sweater from a disapproving relative who's passed on. If the association with the item is a happy, beneficial reminder, by all means keep it, but clearing the clutter that causes us to recall hard times and drags us down can also clear a lot of internal space. A clean and organized living/working space can help encourage an attitude of calm, just on its own.

For those who want to cultivate calm in their environment and don't yet have it, now's a great time to start! Begin the process of simplifying your physical space. I suggest starting with your car, transforming it into a tiny sanctuary. Enjoy the free feeling of a clean car and commit to keeping it that way by penciling "car wash" on your calendar once a month and following through.

Once the car is clean, start in on a small area of your home or work-space: your medicine chest or desk, for example. Take your time, breathe, and slowly make your way through the entire house as you go through the Blueprint, simplifying, donating unneeded items, cleaning and basking in the calm of an organized space. I stand by what my parents told me at least six thousand times: "A place for everything and everything in its place."

My favorite method for maintaining order after the initial organization is to set my timer for five or ten minutes per room once a week or so and complete whatever cleaning and straightening I can in that amount of time, and then move on. It's amazing how much can be accomplished in just a few minutes! I often prioritize tasks by starting with the most disgusting mess and finishing with the least disgusting one—if I've got time for it. This feels more like a game than cleaning house, and knowing I'll only be spending a very specific amount of time cleaning helps me to get started. Sometimes instead of using a timer I'll put on some music and clean each room within the time it takes to listen to a couple of songs. Anything to cultivate a sense of fun!

Resources

Go as "Martha Stewart" as you'd like with organizing your

time and space. Personally speaking, dry-erase calendars, sticky notes and other organizational items put me in a spin of joy—I love that stuff! Just know that some organizational supports are there simply to serve a short-lived purpose or merely as inspiration; they're tools that often fade away when they're no longer needed. It's not a "fail," for instance, if you use sticky notes one month and completely forget about them the next.

Books

Amazon offers an enormous selection of authors ready and willing to help you organize pretty much anything. I've successfully used several books over the years, but donated them to the thrift store during my last book organization! Ha!

I happen to find the delightful and concise little volumes by Darrin Zeer inspiring. His tiny powerhouse, *Office Spa: Stress Relief for the Working Week*, is one of my all-time favorites.

I also highly recommend another short book entitled *The Naturally Clean Home: 150 Super-Easy Herbal Formulas for Green Cleaning*, by Karyn Siegel-Maier. We are typically exposed to a shocking number of toxic chemicals in unnecessary cleaning products daily, and removing these from the home can improve our health and positively impact the wallet as well.

One more old favorite of mine: *The Road Less Traveled: A New Psychology of Love, Traditional Values and Spiritual Growth,* by M. Scott Peck, M.D. I particularly enjoy much of Dr. Peck's discussion of discipline.

Periodicals

I love purchasing a *Real Simple* magazine every once in a while. It's fun to flip through the thick, luxurious pages and ferret out little ideas to organize this or that.

Music

I've got a thing for "relaxation" CDs—typically instrumental music. I pop one in when cleaning and organizing, which lends a spa-like aura to any activity.

Online

As I mentioned, Danielle LaPorte is one of my favorite inspired and inspir*ing* chicks. She blogs, runs programs, writes books and lives her life with the knowledge that she's responsible for her own experience. I suggest finding her online at daniellelaporte.com and checking out what she's got to offer.

Action Three

Selecting a Telescope: Dropping Attention from the Story and Refocusing on the Now

Action Three

Selecting a Telescope: Dropping Attention from the Story and Refocusing on the Now

Serious stargazing requires a quality telescope; selecting one with a high-caliber lens will allow us to clearly view the stars that comprise the constellations in our sky.

If you're practicing relaxation and quiet sitting meditation in Action One and have started using the three interlocking practices in Action Two, cultivating an awareness of choice and of the present moment, you've probably begun to feel a little calmer and more spacious internally, as well as in the physical flow of your daily life. You might also notice while meditating that you're more easily recognizing, acknowledging and then allowing the stream of thoughts to simply be and to quietly move along, placing your attention in your body and on the present moment.

With practice, you will also observe that you're getting better at experiencing emotions rather than resisting, thus permitting them to pass through and eventually lose their power over you. You'll find over time that the flow of mind chatter and degree of emotional volatility may sometimes intensify and at other times may seem to have taken the day off, leaving you in a relatively effortless state of calm.

Keep in mind that no one day with your practices is better or worse or more of a success or failure than another. Continually remind yourself that things don't always have to unfold in ideal or expected ways in order for you to experience calm and begin to connect with your Inner Voice. As previously mentioned, maybe a wonderful surprise interrupts your "ideal" plan and makes your day even *more* ideal... Yay! In any case, if you're genuinely applying the practices, everything that occurs will benefit you in the long run; you'll be learning from all of it. If one day you forget to meditate or catch yourself multitasking, no worries; just let it go and begin again. This is a process. Practicing these new skills in a variety of situations helps integrate them into your daily life, and this is the whole point. There is no perfection to be reached; we simply become more and more present and aware of the joy and freedom available to us in every moment of our daily existence.

The idea of Action Three is to start getting really serious about noticing when we're caught up in thoughts or emotions *outside* of meditation. When we get wound up in thought we're like a bed sheet with a corner stuck in the dryer door, twisting tighter and tighter around itself as the dryer spins. In Action Three we will begin to practice acknowledging, allowing and facilitating the release of extraneous thoughts and recurring emotional patterns in our active lives, just as we do in meditation. We're going to start to get some more clarity on what goes on in our minds on a day-to-day basis.

Now let's open that dryer door.

The Stories We Tell Ourselves

You may notice recurring themes of thought coming and going during the course of your day, just as they do during meditation. You might also observe yourself getting carried away with this thought or that "story." Our minds just keep working, 24/7—even while we sleep. To connect with our Inner Voice, we benefit from the sense of spaciousness that comes with freeing our minds of old patterns, stories and attachments that keep our attention off of the present moment and rooted in the past or future. That holds true whether we're talking about meditation or our regular daily lives.

So What Is This "Story" Business?

The term "story" can apply to a large-scale description of existence, as in your "life story" unfolding. That definition of story is certainly related to the way I use the term in this section. But here I'm more accurately using "story" to refer to the tales we spin in our heads about external occurrences that support beliefs we hold about ourselves and our lives. If this is the first time you've heard the term "story" used in this way, allow me to explain a little further.

When we make assumptions for which we lack supporting concrete evidence, we're making up a "story." When a call to a friend is not returned, for example, and we assume that they're upset with us or are too busy to be bothered, we are simply spinning stories that may have nothing to do with the real reason we haven't yet heard from them. Perhaps the friend is laid up with the stomach flu, her phone has been misplaced, or she's simply out of town with no service. The point is, when we don't *know* what's going on, instead of simply leaving it at that, we tend to make up stories that reflect underlying fears and beliefs. While it is true that if we analyze these stories we may reveal to ourselves what our underlying beliefs are, storytelling nevertheless takes up a lot of time and mental space and clouds our awareness of what's really there. Our aim here is to stop engaging with these tall tales.

Fictions and fantasies may be overlaid onto the past, present or future. This is a mental habit we can train ourselves out of. I'm encouraging you here to start recognizing when storytelling occurs, see it for what it is and thus drop attention from the story, bringing our attention back to the present moment. Stick with the facts of the situation and allow yourself the freedom of releasing attachment to a story or an outcome whenever possible. Just let what is *be*, without predicting, anticipating or judging. Everything else is simply not reality.

Stories: Reliving the Past in the Now

How does this proclivity for telling ourselves stories come about? In part it arises because our brains like to relate one thing to another and detect patterns, perceiving a whole—the gestalt—often when it isn't actually there. Additionally, sometimes even minor incidents in our lives leave us with associations about certain people, groups or situations that we then mistakenly apply as general rules. Also, as we learned in high school science classes, correlation is not causation—although we often act as if it were, developing knee-jerk reactions to events, people or things that are actually unrelated to our assumptions. On top of all that, everyone knows that a little drama often feels exciting, and a good story can be fun to tell! The biggest culprits however, lying at the root of our tendency to overlay assumptions and tell stories about neutral events, are deeply embedded critical past experiences. From these experiences we drew often-erroneous conclusions that solidified into beliefs about ourselves and about life in general, which insidiously weave themselves into the stories we tell ourselves.

These beliefs become our insecurities, often referred to as "limiting beliefs." In the Introduction we discussed how we develop our sense of self and some of the reasons we disconnect from our Inner Voice in the first place. We saw how past experiences can imprint us with illogical and false beliefs about our self-worth. These beliefs may persist into adulthood and perpetuate self-defeating, repetitive patterns of thinking that we are somehow "not good enough." Such limiting beliefs tend to be at the root of the emotions that surface during meditation as well.

Fortunately as adults we're in charge of who we are. We get to (and, I would propose, have a *responsibility* to) examine and let go of untruths, dispelling the power of these limiting beliefs—but we must first become aware of them. If we're on a journey toward inner connection, freedom and a life of our dreams, this process must be high on our priority list.

Letting Go

In Action One we learned how to begin to release emotions and untruths and dispel their powers by working with them in meditation using the Acceptance Process. In Action Three we'll be dealing with them in our active lives in much the same way—*outside* of meditation.

Let me give you an example. In my own life, as I practiced the Actions I'm sharing with you, I began to notice that I experienced emotions around the perception that I was being criticized frequently; that is, I often felt that others were criticizing me when in fact they were doing nothing of the sort. A comment such as, "You got your hair cut!" might trigger hurt or upset, as I interpreted that my haircut was being criticized, for instance, when the person was simply noting that my hair had been trimmed. When I'd turn to a friend who'd also heard the comment, I noticed that they'd often interpreted it completely differently and hadn't heard any criticism at all.

Over time, after observing this pattern surface again and again, whenever I felt I was being criticized I scrutinized the facts. What I discovered was that the interpretation, "I'm being criticized," typically originated from within me and not from the "offending" individual. I recognized my reaction as arising from a limiting belief that I needed others' approval (a version of "I'm not good enough"), about which I also felt a degree of anger and shame.

Using the Acceptance Process in meditation and in my active life, I worked with the misperception that I wasn't just fine the way I was and that I needed approval from others. After some time, this process began to release the hold those old emotions had on me. Now I rarely feel criticized when it's not actually occurring. When I truly am receiving criticism from another, I can now consider its accuracy and make adjustments or disregard it, largely without the old accompanying emotions.

Divesting ourselves of limiting beliefs begins with awareness of our mind-chatter and recurring emotions. This awareness then lays bare our erroneous mind patterns and emotional wounds and shines the light of consciousness on our "stories." While the release of some deep psychological issues is best supported by a professional, many limiting beliefs can often be routed out by observation, a little critical thinking and the conscious and patient re-wiring that occurs through awareness and acceptance of the emotions behind the thoughts.

Stories: Recreating the Past in the Future

Anything we tell ourselves or imagine about the future is by definition a "story" because it hasn't happened! While that story may sometimes reflect the likelihood of a particular outcome based on past experiences, in general, predicting the future is about as accurate as consulting a crystal ball. There's nothing wrong with preparing for moments that have not yet arrived by acting in the present, but if we simply worry or play out old patterns and fail to question the status quo, we perpetuate old ways of being that don't serve us anymore. We forget that our power lies in our ability to live our lives moment by moment; we really can shift out of cruise control and live consciously.

You may have noticed that "stories" or assumptions about future events often prove false. Nine times out of ten, don't you find that what you *imagined* might happen (fainting in the middle of delivering a speech, for example) does not, in fact, occur, and that dreaming all that up was simply a waste of time and energy? Even if the imagined event actually occurs, all we can ever do anyway is deal with whatever is there in the moment and move on. Worrying about all the potential possibilities does nothing to protect us from harm, and can actually be detrimental. I remember once getting a driving lesson from my friend Jeff, a professional race-car driver and racing coach. Just before he put the car into a hard skid by yanking the emergency brake as I drove the practice course, he told me this: "Keep your eyes focused on where you want to go and you will instinctively correct the car in that direction. If you're looking at the pole you might hit, you will hit that pole almost every time. The car will go in the direction you are looking. *Focus on where you want to be*." Amazing life advice as well!

Rewriting the Past

We experience the past as memory and are just as likely to overlay "stories" over past events as we are with future and present ones. In fact, it's even easier to use hindsight to tie events together and explain occurrences as part of repeating themes that support the beliefs we hold about ourselves and the world.

Imagine for a moment that I have a cousin named Chet, with whom I once planned a road trip. Chet, like a lot of other folks, harbors a limiting belief that whispers, "I'm not important." While I may remember only that I went to the store and bought kale chips to take with us on our adventure, thanks to this sinister little belief of his, my fabricated cousin Chet might recall the same event and infuse it with his own "story." "She knows I hate kale! No one ever listens when I talk—she doesn't really care about me!"

While I may have forgotten or not even have known in the first place that Chet despises kale, and I might subsequently have made a different choice had I known or remembered, any actual intention to disrupt Chet's kale-free diet was simply his own "story." His assertion that, "she doesn't care" had nothing to do with me; he's actually very important to me and I love my fake cousin dearly!

It's easy to understand why arguments and disagreements about past events surface all the time. Most of us carry around false beliefs about ourselves and unconsciously look for evidence to support them—and we find it. If we were to look for support for an *opposite* conclusion in identical circumstances, however, we would often find that as well. We're not just observers; we're also fiction writers when it comes not only to our past but to our lives in general. Once we recognize this we can step back and take another look: Fact? Or fiction?

HERE WE GO

In Action Three you will start to pay attention to your thoughts during your active day, observing them just as you're doing in meditation. You will likely notice, as mentioned, how most of them tend toward insignificant chatter and repetitive mental and emotional themes. Observe the way some thoughts grab your attention and escalate into mini soap operas that activate recurring emotional patterns. These are emotions that need to be experienced and allowed to move through and out of our systems. Use the Acceptance Process when they arise.

Start to observe how much of your thinking is cyclical, repetitive and tangential. Your goal in practicing Action Three is to simply notice the thoughts and stories outside of meditation, acknowledge and feel any emotions that come up, and return your focus to the present moment *as soon as you realize you're getting tangled up.* This will assist in bringing you back into the present moment to actually experience your life, while simultaneously clearing more space for your Inner Voice to come through.

NOTE: Don't be concerned that you'll have to drop an important thought. No way! The idea here is simply to be able to catch yourself in and detach from automatic emotional reactions, stories and mind-eddies when you want to. You'll be keeping your Mini IV Notebook with you at all times so that, just like in meditation, when a thought that you *want* to remember hits you,

you can write it down and move on with your day. Remember: thinking can obviously be a very useful tool, but as Eckhart Tolle points out, we want to make sure we're using *it*, instead of it using *us*.

Materials

- IV Notebook
- Mini IV Notebook
- Writing utensil
- Reminder item: any item you can place on your person daily that will be visible to you when you're wearing it, such as a watch, ring, bracelet, etc. (A necklace, for example, won't work.)

Time

Several moments during your active day.

HOW

Essentially you'll be reminding yourself to practice Action Three during the day, noticing and then dropping attention from mind chatter and stories and bringing your focus back to the here and now. As discussed, make use of the Acceptance Process as emotions grab hold of you during the day. As you decrease the power your emotions wield and release focus from unnecessary tangential thought, you might start to feel like you've actually *freed up* some mental time and space to relax in. Notice when that occurs and enjoy it!

Let's keep this process really, really simple.

1. Wear your chosen reminder item daily.

2. Every time you catch sight of that item during your day, notice and then drop your attention from any repetitive thoughts or stories that might be circulating Accept and feel any emotions that present themselves and remind yourself to focus attention on the task at hand, the environment or the person in front of you. I like to silently say, "here," just as I do in meditation.

You'll be experiencing what's actually happening, staying present and aware, and letting go of a lot of unnecessary stories your brain wants to concoct. See how many times a day you can simply return to what's going on right in front of you at the moment. When you drop a line of thinking, come back to your surroundings, to what you're physically experiencing at that moment. Feel the breeze on your arms, the sun on your face, the steering wheel in your hand, your rump on the chair; simply return to the here and now.

3. Notice how you feel about completing the above practice during the day. What effect does it have on how you feel? Each day, jot down any experiences you find interesting or enlightening in your IV Notebook. Keep your Mini IV Notebook with you at all times in case you encounter thoughts you feel are important enough to take note of and deal with at an appropriate time.

4. Pay particular attention to and record recurring mental and emotional patterns that start to emerge as you become conscious of and familiar with your internal experiences. When you begin to watch yourself and observe your stories, look closely at which limiting beliefs those stories might be supporting and what the core emotions behind them are. Work with those guys, if at all possible, right when they come up by staying present and allowing the emotions. The more you deal with these emotions on the spot, the more quickly they'll lose their power over you.

5. When you sit down at the end of the day, prior to meditation, review your Mini IV Notebook and schedule any necessary actions.

New You: Way Cooler Than Old You

Okay! Now let me give you a couple of examples of situations you might encounter, contrasting Old You (the you before you met Action Three), to New You (the you who's learning to drop unnecessary attachments to thoughts, stories and emotions clogging your system).

Example 1

Old You (waiting in the parking lot at the grocery store): "Aaargh! That guy just snaked my parking spot! I saw it first! Look at his stupid muscle car... OMG... If he thinks he can just waltz in there and... So rude!... Let's see how he likes this!" Hoooooooooonk! (Emotional Response: Irritation/Anger)

New You: "That dude just took my spot! Oh, wait a minute... I notice I'm getting caught up in this '*my* parking spot' story and letting it run away with my peace of mind. Is it really true? Who cares? This is so not important." Notice, allow and observe your emotions.

Then...

Drop it. "No big deal, I'll find somewhere else to park." (Emotional Response: Calm).

This process can be as simple as a quick observation and acknowledgement, or it might include sitting in your car in the parking lot and going through the Acceptance Process when you detect an emotional reaction; it need only take a few moments. You can continue to stay present with any residual emotions while you shop as well.

Example 2

Old You (unexpectedly running into a friend you haven't seen in a few weeks): "Oh crap, there's Rhonda. I forgot to call her back last week. I bet she's mad. She never calls ME back though! Ugh I wish I could just avoid her..." (Emotional Response: Anxiety/Irritation).

New You: "There's Rhonda—I forgot to return her call... Shoot! I bet she's not happy with *me*... Now hold on! I'm making assumptions and creating a story here, really running away with it!

Is this really true? Who *knows* what she's thinking!" Notice, allow and observe your emotions.

Then…

Drop it. "I'll just say hi and apologize for not calling back, no big deal. I can always talk out anything that comes up with her. Drama-free!" (Emotional Response: Calm/Openness).

See how not getting caught up in your mind's chatter, dropping attention from stories and just coming back to the moment encourages calm and openness rather than angst, wasted energy and closed-off feelings?

A Quick Aside About Calm Internal Presence

As mentioned in Action One regarding calm *during* meditation, calm internal presence *outside* of meditation means that we actually feel and experience calm. It does not mean "keeping our cool" or acting calm when we feel anything *but* inside. Calm internal presence isn't something we practice; it's what naturally occurs when we consistently acknowledge what's real for us— allowing, accepting and working with whatever shows up— internally and externally, returning again and again to the present moment.

More About the New You

As you start to put these first three Actions into practice, pretty soon you'll notice some changes in your demeanor and general attitude. Don't be surprised if people around you start to peer at you out of the corners of their eyes and ask what you're doing differently. Deep down, most people just truly want to be happy, and the joy and calm that seep through the gaps that appear when excess mental chatter and storytelling dissipate will become apparent to others. They'll want to know what you're doing so they can do it too.

Expect your social life to rev up as well! Let's get real: *you'd* probably rather hang out with New You than Old You, am I right? And who wouldn't?! New You—arriving on time, relaxed, knowing your priorities for the day, paying attention to the present moment and rolling with the punches—actually gets to *savor* running into an old friend unexpectedly. New You, no longer frazzled or distracted by mind chatter and meaningless fictions, really listens and shares—in the moment.

New You obviously makes a much better friend, employee, spouse... everything! New You deals with issues consciously, at appropriate times, rather than constantly brain-spinning. New You pays attention and gets to *experience* what's happening in front of you, whether it's hiking a trail with your dog or creating a delectable soufflé. New You genuinely listens when your friends talk and, because of that, responds authentically as well. Everyone appreciates being truly seen and heard; New You can give this gift to everyone you come in contact with. New You also gets to avoid a good portion of the anxiety, irritation, exhaustion and upset that unnecessary internal chatter, storytelling and expectations bring up during the day. New You relaxes and breathes.

In short, New You is really and truly *living*, which is nothing short of awesome.

Challenging Arenas

Feeling like you've got all of this stuff mastered and want to take it up a notch? As Ram Dass suggests, take a trip to see your family!

Dropping attention from thoughts and emotional patterns with our family of origin tends to be difficult for most people. Family is where our deepest ties lie, and habits within that structure often trigger old beliefs and behavior patterns. But on the other hand, it's a great place to practice your new skills!

In general, the closer our connection to an individual, the greater the chance we'll encounter deeply embedded resistance within ourselves when we interact with them. For one, we have more to "lose" in these relationships—these are our roots. Family members in particular may be fairly comfortable spouting off an unflattering interpretation of us or our behavior, and acting differently with them may incite reactions we'd prefer to avoid. On the other hand, we may find relatives surprisingly interested and supportive!

Often looking to maintain their own identities through complex relationship dynamics, however, family members (as well as other people with whom we have close relationships) can unconsciously tend toward expressing an investment in our continuing to enact past roles rather than making any self-discoveries or significant growth. Why? Our changes may upset the dynamics of the current relationship and/or unintentionally invite the other party to question their own behavior or beliefs. This is sometimes an unwelcome invitation.

Family *is* a great training ground, but know that it will probably also be your toughest arena—your own personal Thunderdome. Our interactions with family and significant others illuminate for us in big, bold, neon letters where we're still holding onto limiting beliefs and getting wound up in resistant thought patterns and emotions, like that sheet in the dryer. It's okay; it will keep you humble, and humble is a good thing. Remember that these practices are not about being in control. They're about really experiencing ourselves and our perceived limitations in the moment so that we can enter any areas of difficulty, process them and eventually regain our joy and freedom. Sometimes it just takes time for others to adjust to our new ways of being, and authentic actions can and often do deepen and strengthen healthy relationships. Other situations, however, may result in a dramatic shift in the form of the relationship or in extreme cases, the release of an unhealthy relationship altogether.

If you find yourself regressing to childhood behavior, thoughts and emotional patterns when visiting your family, don't despair. You're certainly not alone. It doesn't mean you're not getting this stuff or it's not "working." It just means you're human and that those old patterns run very deep, as they do for all of us.

Keep in mind also that the idea here, by being entirely present, is to infuse our entire lives with this ability to *observe* rather than be *consumed* by our thoughts and emotions, so that in as much of our lives as possible we rediscover our calm internal presence. Within that calm presence is the door to our Inner Voice and the freedom to truly experience our lives, making choices moment by moment with the guidance of our inner wisdom.

Expansion

Amp up the ways in which you remind yourself to drop attention from stories and bring yourself back into the present moment. Here are a few ideas to get you started:

1. Set your phone alarm to go off every hour. When it does, notice and then drop attention from any circulating stories and bring yourself back into the now. Then reset and repeat.

2. Text a friend you've recruited as a "presence buddy" to bring yourself back to the present moment. The text can be a simple "Present!" or "You here?" sent off a couple of times a day.

3. Designate a certain color as your "presence" reminder—every time you notice something green, for example, that's your cue to be present!

4. Same as above, but use a common animal (a dog, for instance) or a specific kind of car to remind you to snap back into awareness of the present moment.

I'm sure you can think of other creative reminders. Remember that gaining mastery with this skill really is a matter of practice!

Guerilla Story-Free

Here's something fun that can really accelerate an awareness of the tendency we have to tell ourselves stories that support our limiting beliefs. As you become aware of a story you're spinning about an event, drop attention from it. Then consider the limiting belief behind it, which will always be some version of "I'm not good enough." In the Rhonda encounter, the limiting belief would have been something along the lines of "I don't live up to others' expectations of me. I'm not good enough." Now, just for fun, make up a new story based on precisely the *opposite* belief about yourself—namely, that you're positively great just the way you are. Using the interaction with Rhonda (from the New You examples above) to illustrate this point, you might "assume" that Rhonda thinks you're an incredibly inspiring and wonderful human being who's been very busy with that wonderful life of yours. She's probably overjoyed to see you—she's missed you SO much and can't WAIT to get together again!

Notice how both versions are just stories? It doesn't matter if they're spun positively or negatively. You'll find out how Rhonda feels when you interact with her, and you'll address that if you need to when the time comes. With this approach, you'll be engaging with what's really there and thus dealing with it appropriately, instead of reacting to a fantasy in your head.

The key is that our stories reveal to us our underlying beliefs about ourselves, beliefs that are often false and unrelated to actual circumstances. When we connect with our Inner Voice, illuminate and drop old thought patterns, we become aware that quite often our assumptions about people's thoughts and feelings regarding us are simply *our own* erroneous projected beliefs about *ourselves*. Among other benefits, this knowledge eventually simplifies our relationship with ourselves and with others.

Resources

Books

The Power of Now: A Guide to Spiritual Enlightenment by Eckhart
   Tolle
Remember, Be Here Now by Ram Dass
Loving What Is: Four Questions That Can Change Your Life by
   Byron Katie

Action Four

Readying the Equipment:
Physical Call and Response

Action Four

Readying the Equipment: Physical Call and Response

Telescope in hand, we locate an excellent spot for viewing and begin to set up. The weather is calm, and soon it will be dark. We must take the time now to attend to our equipment, readying it and ourselves for stargazing.

Now it's time for some fun! In Action Four we'll focus on our physical experience. I'll encourage you to become more aware of the information your physical sensations relay to you moment by moment so that you will:

- Become more deeply acquainted with what your body is telling you about your internal state.
- Get in touch with your five senses, increasing your awareness of your environment.
- Recognize the importance of consistently responding to your body's messages.

Keep in mind that even though we're adding layers to your practice, they're gossamer layers that will continue to open up space and time for you. With Action Four you'll learn to stay physically regulated, and to stop and smell the roses. Sounds simple, but like everything here, it actually takes some practice for most folks! I know it did for me. From here you'll begin to experience more tranquility and increased energy, clearing the path to connection to self, and hence, to your intuitive power.

Unless you play a sport, dance, or otherwise integrate

movement into your daily life, it's sometimes easy to forget that our bodies are there at all. Many folks hunker down in a cubicle with their coffee in the morning and emerge, eight hours later, stiff and cranky, having ignored their bodies all day long. Even if we conscientiously schedule regular massages, facials or chiropractic appointments, they're no substitute for tuning in to our body's moment-by-moment cues. In fact, you may find that these kinds of treatments are required less often as you start consistently listening and responding to your body's messages. This is a commonsense way to keep ourselves in tip-top condition.

In my own life, I regularly spend long periods of time in front of the computer screen. Even though I have the freedom to take a break whenever I need to, I initially found it necessary to train myself to tune in to my body periodically and adjust my posture, grab a snack or a glass of water, and stretch. That tuning in and responding part is where we're headed right now.

As human animals, our ability to shut out the outside world and live large chunks of time in our heads allows us to invent jet engines, immerse ourselves in Kung-Fu movies or plan a European vacation. The intellect is generally highly valued in our culture, often over (and sometimes to the exclusion of) the many other aspects of who we are as human beings. We all know we're more than just our brains, but as our mental capacities often play starring roles in our careers and day-to-day lives, we're apt to neglect ourselves as *physical* beings. I'm not just talking about putting on a few pounds or forgetting to floss; I'm also referring to the tendency to ignore the little signals our bodies send us all day long. Many of us are so tuned-out that we don't notice our bodies unless they're screaming at us—usually when we're in pain.

Are you starting to dread that I'm about to instruct you to hightail it to the gym six days a week? Fear not! While, yes, I encourage anyone interested in their own well-being to get out there and *move*, that's not where I'm going with Action Four. My aim here is simply to encourage you to begin listening and responding to your body's messages. Why? Because the ability to perceive and respond to our physical sensations is key to tuning in to the Inner Voice. Your Inner Voice will communicate with you via those same messages—through feelings and physical sensations. With increasing awareness of ourselves as whole beings, our awareness of the Inner Voice will also expand. Not to mention that if we neglect one part of ourselves, the whole operates on a lower level. We build trust in our true self's competency one instinctual nudge at a time, and that starts with listening to our physical internal communication systems.

So What Does it Mean to "Listen to My Body?"

Good question. Optimally, listening to our bodies means "being in" them consistently, always keeping some of our mental awareness focused internally on our physical experience. At the very least, listening to our bodies means regularly "checking in" with ourselves regarding our physical state.

What signals is the body sending when I check in? Do I feel thirsty? Hungry? Tired? Stiff? Ask yourself whether or not you've been perceiving and responding to these little messages, ignoring them altogether, or somewhere in between. Some people are more tuned in than others, but if these messages are totally off your radar, this Action is going to be an eye-opener for you.

Though we can all become absorbed in thought or activities and periodically override our awareness of physical sensations, training ourselves to check in with how we're doing physically is über important. If we listen and respond to messages fairly consistently, our bodies keep us regulated, we're not distracted by sensations we've ignored, we can think clearly and we *feel good*. This in turn allows us to focus our attention on the present moment—the only moment in which we have access to our Inner Voice. Underlying hunger, freezing feet or overdue bathroom breaks diffuse our focus and weaken our strength for accomplishing whatever it is we need to do, not to mention just flat out spoiling our fun. If we ignore our inner communication or don't perceive it in the first place, it's easy to end up with a nasty woops-I-forgot-to-eat headache, a stiff neck from sitting in one position too long, or jelly-brain after ignoring our bedtime too many nights in a row.

If you're someone who relies almost exclusively on outside cues for regulation like I was, this Action will help you understand what it means to trust yourself on a basic level. If you eat or sleep only when the clock tells you to, for instance, you're now going to start to tune in to when you actually *experience* sleepiness and hunger, no matter what the clock says. If you count on your doctor to tell you when to exercise and what to eat, get ready to transfer that responsibility onto yourself. I'm certainly not suggesting we don't need doctors or alarm clocks; I'm simply bringing it to your attention that if we listen to ourselves we find that when we're healthy our bodies are their own best friends. They know what's in their best interest. Even doctors only facilitate the body's own power to heal itself; your body does all the real work.

Did you know that your body will guide you to exercise and rest when it needs to? If we get clear enough, it will even tell us what foods it needs. If you practice paying attention to physical signals, you won't need to worry about getting enough water or overeating either; your body will let you know what it needs to stay healthy. The trick is that you have to tune in, listen to it and act. You know that little voice that pipes up when you cut a second piece of cake or agree to go out late *again*? Or how about that craving for fresh fruit after you've been ill? Start paying attention—that voice knows what it's talking about. Tune in and commit to listening.

Our Bodies: Finely-Tuned Monitoring Systems

Neurologists inform us that the brain is the last frontier and that we're only just beginning to scratch the surface of understanding its complex functions. As we know, the body and brain work together as part of a single intelligent system, diligently and efficiently maintaining homeostasis at all times, constantly monitoring the ways in which we respond internally and externally to our environment. Amazing. And all this, mind you, without any input from our conscious selves.

What's my point? As physical beings, we always have access to the wisdom of this incredibly knowledgeable and integrated system. This system will guide us to a higher quality of life and back to ourselves *if we listen to it*. If we tune in to our physical selves, not only will we more likely avoid body breakdowns such as illness and disease, we will also gain access to a world of health, guided by our own internal physician, dietitian and personal trainer. What's not to love?

So How Do We Tune In?

The general idea is as follows: first, we slow down, focus our attention on the present moment, and "inhabit" our bodies, by which I mean we cultivate an awareness of our physical sensations. Doing this settles us internally and provides us the chance to come into alignment with our bodies. If we take this opportunity to tune in to and respect our body's cues, we get to breathe, look around, and live in the here and now.

Ahhhhh...

Okay. Let's get into some detail and explore how all of this works.

Start with the obvious stuff. Feel cold? Grab a sweater—*now*. Getting too dark to read? Turn on the light—really, right now. Hungry? Down a handful of nuts. Pronto. Believe me, giving yourself what you need *when you need it* is a habit not many of us employ. Most of us are waaaaay out of practice and have no idea how ignoring these cues effectively deafens us to our Inner Voice.

But, you may ask, am I ever going to get anything *done* if I'm constantly running around for water and sweaters and handfuls of nuts?

Trust me: you'll be fine. In fact, you'll be *more* than fine—you'll be better than ever because you'll be addressing your needs as they arise instead of dealing with the compounded consequences of ignoring them. It's exactly the same as addressing little issues in a relationship as they occur rather than letting them pile up and then exploding at your partner later. Making frequent small adjustments to stay on course while piloting a plane is preferable to sitting back and then making huge corrections to avoid colliding with a mountain or other aircraft later. You get the point: letting things go can result in dire consequences.

Responding to your physical cues is a healthy habit. The more you tune in to yourself, the more you'll start to live in a way that easily provides for your needs on a day-to-day basis. You'll actually begin to recognize and assuage your physical needs more and more easily, and you'll feel better and better. As meeting your own needs becomes second nature, the time and effort involved in doing so actually lessens, and responses continually become more streamlined, simplified and automatic.

An example: Let's say you notice that every day at work, about 10:30 in the morning, your stomach starts growling. For the first several days of observing and acting on this, you run to the vending machine and purchase a small bag of almonds. Then it occurs to you that if you simply placed a large bag of almonds in your desk you could grab a few whenever you needed to. So you do.[10]

Can you see how meeting your needs sorts itself out, simplifies itself and becomes less time consuming as you go along? Furthermore, in the above example, you'll also be avoiding the brain drag that happens when you don't eat, which causes productivity at work to go down, negatively impacts your immune system, and plops you directly in the path of this season's flu.

But seriously, is grabbing a handful of nuts when your stomach grumbles really all that important? Absolutely. Every time you ignore these little messages, you further bully the Inner Voice and put more distance between you and your inner wisdom. Conversely, every time you listen to and act on inner communication, you strengthen the bond with your inner guide. That's why you picked up this book, isn't it?

All This Pampering Myself! Won't I Gain Weight and Get Lazy?

First of all, "pampering" is just an arbitrary judgment of a neutral event, and coddling yourself is not what this is about. All you're doing is responding to your body's signals, and all *they're* doing is telling you what your body needs to stay in optimal operating condition. Don't worry about overeating or over-relaxing. If you're following the Blueprint Actions, you won't over-*any*thing. Here's an example that illustrates why:

Overeating, like most addictive-type behaviors, generally happens for one of the following reasons:

- We ignore our hunger pangs and then binge when we finally have access to food.

---

[10] Keep in mind that in the interest of encouraging health on all levels, I suggest responding with healthy options, such as almonds, rather than a bag of potato chips.

- We're not present and simply stuff food in our mouths unconsciously.
- We want to distract ourselves from feeling pain resulting from underlying stories about not being good enough, and we stuff those emotions down with food.

Hey, look at that! We've already addressed those underlying issues in Actions One through Four in the Blueprint! While habits aren't easy to break and addictions are even tougher, in general, implementing the Actions will greatly reduce the tendency to engage in overdoing on anything. If you need extra help, by all means get it—but we're on the right track here. When we're truly *present*, to ourselves and to our environment, we respond to the current moment out of immediate awareness rather than from unconscious habit or fear. Learn to trust your body. Once it comes back into balance, it will literally provide a healthy return on your investment.

NOTE: As you begin to tune in to yourself physically, you may start to notice discomforts you weren't paying attention to before, such as shoulder soreness from sitting in one position too long. This is a good thing! You may have been drowning out the signals your body was giving you previously. Listen to your body and give it what it needs. If you're thinking, "but I'd rather ignore them—I actually prefer *not* to feel those aches and pains," don't kid yourself; they'll get you sooner or later. Like emotions, if you let these signals continue without acknowledging and addressing them, they only persist, growing louder and more painful. Repeatedly ignoring your body's polite "Psst... Hey, um, a little help over here please..." may land you a major illness or injury instead of a minor discomfort.

Does the idea of taking care of yourself *still* make you feel selfish? Let's turn that idea on its head once and for all.

Could Ignoring Our Inner Messages Actually Be Selfish And Irresponsible?

Yes! Who is responsible for you? If you're over eighteen and able-bodied, there's only one answer to that question: *you*. If you don't listen to and act on your own inner guidance system when it tells you exactly what your body needs, who will?

If you ignore the "check engine" light and your car breaks down, whose fault is that? Is it irresponsible to ignore that light? Yes. Why would you ignore it? "I'm too busy, I'm late, it's such a hassle..." Sound familiar? "I'd like to eat better but I don't have the time to make healthy food." "Sure I want to exercise but I don't want to deal with joining a gym." Get ready for some time in the repair shop!

While accidents, illness and health conditions can certainly strike out of the blue regardless of personal habits, what I'm talking about here are avoidable health consequences resulting from a lack of self-care.

Have you ever been laid up with a cold after pushing yourself too hard? For me it was respiratory infections and migraines that would force me to take some time off. Your body's number one priority is your health; it doesn't care about project deadlines or red-eye flights. If you continue to push it and ignore its cues, your body gives you louder and louder signals until you have no choice but to give it a break and allow it the time and energy it needs to repair itself. Our bodies work so hard for us and they deserve our care and respect. By taking Action Four seriously you will actually save yourself real pain and suffering in the future.

What we often don't consider is that sloughing off responsibility for addressing our physical symptoms by burying our heads in the sand doesn't always affect only us. Time off work, sick time in bed away from our families, or spreading a cold we haven't addressed are only a few examples of the ways in which our choice to ignore our inner messages and physical symptoms affects others in a negative way.

It doesn't help that in our culture people are often socially rewarded for overworking, denying themselves care and eventually ending up sick (and then going to *work* sick). For some reason, some people think martyrdom is acceptable. You know what? I disagree. It isn't brave, it isn't good, and it isn't selfless—it's exactly the opposite. People who take responsibility for themselves and their lives take care of themselves and are thus able to bring their best selves to whomever and whatever they encounter. Everyone benefits from that.

Imagine how great it would be if the majority of the folks you came into contact with felt healthy and good *because they took care of themselves*! The world would be a very different place. People who feel good pass that good, happy feeling on to everyone they come in contact with. Choose to take care of yourself and be one of those people who contributes to the "happy" in other people's days. The truth is, no matter how important your job is, how many people rely on you and how high-up your position is, you can *absolutely* take a bathroom break, get a drink of water and stretch your legs when you need to—and probably take a sick day or two when that's required.

Though most of us are guilty of dragging our under-the-weather selves to work at one time or another, myself included (giving up a day of acting is one of my least favorite things!), taking time off is the responsible thing to do, particularly if you work with children or the elderly. For whatever reason, if you absolutely won't take the day off, then do everything you can to take care of yourself while you're at work—bring tea and a healthy snack, perhaps, take frequent breaks and rest your eyes at lunchtime—and try to limit your contact with co-workers.

The Five Senses—Paying Attention to the World Outside

If we're not fully experiencing the world with our five senses, we're literally missing out on much of the incredible joy and wonder of being alive. The scent of a rosemary bush, the sight of a shooting star, the sound of crows calling to each other overhead and the soft texture of a new leaf... All these things and more go unnoticed if we're not paying attention to the signals our bodies are receiving and sending. Sure, there's also the aroma of cat poop and the peaceful serenity of leaf blowers, but that's part of life too!

In these instances, the signals our bodies are sending us are our perceptions of the external world. If we're too distracted, busy or frazzled, much of the sensual experiences of life simply go unnoticed; they just don't register. To truly experience the richness of our existence, we want to encourage awareness of the present moment and receive the sensations arising from our insanely awesome and highly attuned physical selves.

Connecting with nature can be key in grounding ourselves and getting back to a space where we're settled and in tune with our world. Being in and aware of nature resets our systems, relaxing and recharging us. If you can start to spend a little more time in nature, do it—you won't regret it. For most of us, nature is pretty much everywhere if we're tuned in and looking for it, and we don't have to plan a trip to Yosemite to find it. I often spot squirrels, rabbits, birds of all kinds, raccoons and of course cats and dogs on my daily walks, not to mention a gorgeous array of trees, grasses, flowers and shrubs. And I live in Los Angeles!

An Integrated Whole

Both aspects of the internal awareness we've discussed—what our bodies relay to us about their internal state and what they tell us about our external environment—are really an integrated whole. Attuning to one will increase awareness of the other as well. Our sensations comprise the crucial conduit through which we experience life—and our Inner Voice. Our bodies are our tools, our operating system, and the instrument through which we play our music. The more in tune we are with them, the healthier they and we, will be.

HERE WE GO

In Action Four, we'll be listening to our bodies and paying attention to what they have to say about what's going on inside and outside of us. Then, if action is required, we'll respond.

Simple? Sure, when you get the hang of it! Checking in and being in the present moment, in addition to respecting the messages we hear, is a matter of practice.

Materials

- Your IV Notebook
- Writing utensil
- Watch, rubber band or hairband (for your wrist) or other "reminder" item. This may be any object you choose daily as you dress in the morning. You can add a new reminder item or use the one you've already got in play.
- Optional: camera or camera phone

Time

An initial few minutes to pre-think and plan for physical needs that might arise during the day.

Any time you remember throughout the day, focus your attention on your senses and sensations.

HOW

During your active day (every day):

1. You've been completing the body-energy awareness exercise in meditation. Now you'll bring this practice into your active life several times per day. Pick a time when you'll tune in, perhaps practicing this skill each time you sit down in your car before starting the engine, or when sitting down to each meal, or the moment before answering or making a phone call. Maybe use a reminder item or place a sticker on your car mirror or phone to cue you to take a moment to tune in and feel your body's energy. It only takes a couple of seconds.

2. In the beginning, if it's easier for you, choose only one part of your body to focus on (your palms or the bottoms of your feet, for example). Feel the energy there instead of feeling it throughout your entire body. This awareness practice will bring you back to the present moment whenever you need it to.

3. Pay attention to when you feel hungry, thirsty, tired, itchy etc., and address those needs. If you find it doesn't occur to you to check in with your body regularly, use an alarm (set it to go off every hour or so) or your visual reminder (ring, etc.) to cue you. Do a little thinking ahead. Place a sweater and your gym bag in the trunk of your car or pack a snack box and a water bottle to keep in your desk at work. Consider items that might be helpful to have immediately on hand and keep them at the ready.

4. Get out there and experience all your five senses have to share with you. Practice focusing your awareness on all the

sensational stuff that populates our world! Literally stop to smell the roses, the candles on the mantel, your food as you prepare and eat it. Experience the texture of your shirt, the warmth and furry-ness of your cat as she sits on your lap. Listen to the subtle sounds around you that may have previously eluded your perception. *Definitely* peer nerdily at tiny insects, the sheen of a leaf and the way the light bounces off a drop of water.

5. Take a walk around your neighborhood and see how many things you can notice that you never paid attention to before. Bring a camera or camera phone if that sounds like fun. Enjoy finding patterns, creatures and flowers and snap some photos. Post these on social media or share them with family members or friends if you like. Spread the fun—it really is infectious!

6. Note any particularly fascinating observations as you start to pay more attention to your world. Write and/or doodle drawings in your IV Notebook, paste or tape pictures or jot down lyrics in a new section entitled something like, "Amazing Things I Noticed." Record anything interesting that you heard, touched, tasted, saw or smelled.

Expansion

Choose four or five songs on Pandora or your iPod (or just use the radio). Set aside fifteen to twenty minutes of private time and boogie your behind off at your own private dance party—just you and your music. This isn't just any dance party though! Instead of reenacting old high school dance moves, listen to the music and allow your body to be moved by it, inspired simply by how you feel when those notes hit your ears. This isn't a performance; it's an experiment! See how physically in tune with the music you can be and let the music flow through you.

One of my favorite things to do is pretend that I actually know how to contemporary dance. I often enact a dramatic number in the middle of my living room by myself. I also put the four hip-hop dance moves I remember from my six months of classes to good use if I'm in that kind of mood. Have fun! The purpose of this activity is to tune in to what you're hearing, notice how it makes you feel and allow your body to take over and respond to the music. If you really allow yourself to let go you'll get a supercharged experience of tuning in to your body from the inside by allowing it to move the way it wants to. I love these private, individual dance parties. When I get tired of working at my desk, it's not uncommon at all for me to pull up YouTube and dance it out for a song or two!

Guerilla Awareness

Plan a morning, afternoon or entire day in nature—maybe a nearby hike or park picnic. Think ahead regarding physical needs that will likely occur: might you need a lunch, a jacket, an extra snack or a sun hat? When you arrive, concentrate on what your senses relay to you. Listen to the birds, feel the pine needles crunch under your feet, and breathe in the scent of sap and sunbaked leaves. Bring your IV Notebook and choose a leaf, a flower, a sugar packet from the restaurant on the way back or something else that will remind you of this trip. Before placing it in your IV Notebook, study it intently—the colors, shapes, aromas, textures— really experience the object itself. Make sure you check in with yourself during the entire trip and meet the physical needs you experience throughout the day. It's an Action Four mini boot camp!

Resources

Books

I suggest further exploring any of the topics we've touched on in this Action: nature, body awareness, the five senses, or anything else that sounds interesting. See what your local library, bookstore, or Amazon has to offer. I particularly enjoy anything about nature, especially animals. Here are a few I like:

Animals, Our Return to Wholeness by Penelope Smith
*Reconnecting with Nature: Finding Wellness through Restoring
    Your Bond with the Earth* by Michael J. Cohen

California Wildlife Viewing Guide by Jeanne L. Clark (I'll bet each
state has a wildlife guide you can pick up)
Biomimicry: Innovation Inspired by Nature by Janine Benyus.
She's also got a great Ted Talk on this subject you can find
online as well.

Friend plug: I also especially love the yoga photo how-to
section in my friend Michelle Paisley's book, *Yoga for a Broken
Heart: A Spiritual Guide to Healing from Break-up, Loss, Death or
Divorce.* It's a goodie.

Videos

To get yourself tuned in to your body there's nothing like a
little easy yoga. Rodney Yee has an AM/PM DVD out that I
picked up at my local co-op. I've used the morning section off and
on for years (I don't really love the evening portion—I'm just not
that flexible). It's a very simple set of poses that take about twenty
minutes to move through. If you find you like the stretching
portion of this practice, feel free to expand it into whatever you'd
like, but just focus on how it feels, not on accomplishing the poses
perfectly.

Online programs, Apps and Low Tech Reminders

Much of the challenge of this Action's practice, like all of the
Actions, is simply to remember to do it. Little computer programs
and apps exist that will alert you every so often to check in with
yourself (*GPS For the Soul* is one I like). You can also set the
alarm on your phone (or stove, if you're at home, or whatever you
have available) to go off every hour or so. When the alarm goes
off, stop what you're doing and tune into your body. Feel the chair,
your shoes against your feet, whether you're hot or cold, etc.
Check in. This takes five to ten seconds and will get you in the
habit of becoming aware and present, touching base with what
your body is telling you.

Now, set this book down, check in and go get that snack, take
that stretch break or use the restroom—whatever you need to do!

Action Five

Pinpoints of Light:
Attuning to Joy

Action Five

Pinpoints of Light: Attuning to Joy

This is where we begin to look up to the sky and notice that hey, there are a myriad of little lights up there! Those pinpoints of light are our guiding stars—the activities, people, places and things that energize or deplete us.

Ready to take a giant leap ahead in your journey back to yourself? Perfect.

You're getting the basics down, listening for and responding to physical and sense communications; that's your foundation. In Action Five we're going to expand on that idea. Using the same process we employed in Action Four to tune in to what our bodies are sensing and telling us (bringing ourselves into the present and checking in with how we're feeling), we're going to take it deeper. Now we're going to pay attention to what *energizes* us, and conversely, to what *depletes* us of energy. What the heck does that mean?

Some of you will immediately understand what I'm talking about when I describe "feeling energized" and "feeling depleted" and may in fact already be able to list several things, people, locations or activities that either make you feel good or zap your energy when you're engaged with them. For others, this may be a completely foreign concept, and that's just fine—you're not alone, and this chapter is for you, too! After this Action, no matter where you're starting, you'll have a much better idea of what I'm talking about and will start to get the hang of picking up on what's energizing for you and what isn't. Let's start with some good old-fashioned definitions!

Energized

Feeling energized is exactly what it sounds like—when engaging with a task, person or place, etc., you experience a sense of gaining energy you didn't have before. Pay attention to your body and it will tell you whether something is energizing, depleting or neutral for you. You might experience "energized" as feeling good, delighted, light, or free. You'll feel a sense of possibility, expansiveness, openness and interest.

When you feel energized, it's immediately apparent to those around you. If they're paying attention, they'll describe your face or eyes as "lit up." They might say something like, "Wow, when you started talking about classical music, your face just lit up!" And it really does; you can feel it yourself once you learn how to tune in. Keep an ear out for those kinds of comments from others, and listen for your own voice picking up intensity when you hit on certain topics. Feeling energized feels *good*. When you're energized you're animated (even if it's primarily internal), refreshed and engaged with what's going on in the present moment; you're experiencing heightened awareness and enjoying it.

Also pay attention to your actions—do you hop up to a particular friend's door two steps at a time? Whistle as you open up the newspaper to the crossword on Sunday morning? These clues let you know you're looking forward to or enjoying what you're doing or about to do. Physical signs of feeling energized might include alert eye gaze, upright posture, increased physicality (such as bustin' a move), and facing or leaning toward the activity or person with both head and body; posture and body language will indicate engagement and enjoyment. When I leave the gym, I sometimes skip to my car—I'm so energized that I've just got to *move!* If you're really tuned in to it, the feeling of being energized is synonymous with joy.

Feeling energized can also be experienced as just "being yourself." Let me clarify. If you've ever felt really stressed, done something to recharge (such as take a nap or get a massage) and then felt better, you might describe feeling better as "feeling like myself again." Isn't it interesting that we actually refer to activities that reinvigorate us as "recharging" or even say we're "recharging our batteries"? Energy is not just a metaphor; it's something you will physically experience in your body once you're really tuned in.

On a very simple level, before you go to sleep at night after a long day you may experience feeling tired and depleted, and in the morning after a good sleep you'll feel energized again.

Depleted

Feeling depleted means experiencing a sense of being drained of energy; energy is sucked out of you. When you're depleted, you'll feel zapped of your interest or desire to engage with what's going on. Something that depletes you of energy might feel tiring, dark, boring, heavy or dense. It may come with a sense of "yuck" in the area of your stomach, sometimes along with a tightness in the chest; it will feel restrictive.

Just like they do when we feel energized, our actions will clue us in to when we feel depleted as well. Though we're often simply feeling depleted by something that cannot actually physically harm us (someone yammering on endlessly about themselves, for example, as opposed to a tiger jumping at us), signs of depletion often take the form of physical actions that symbolically or literally shield us from what's happening. These signs may include averting eye gaze, hunching up shoulders, turning the head or body away, and slouching or leaning against something. Feeling depleted causes you to shut down inside to what's going on and to focus on getting away from the situation, whether that retreat comes in the form of a mental escape (daydreaming, for example) or an actual physical disconnection (breaking eye contact, walking away, hanging up the phone, etc.).

When I used to work in a job that I didn't like all that much, it sapped my energy all day long. By the end of the day I had a headache and tunnel vision; I couldn't wait to jump into my car and head home. Once I pulled out of the parking lot, I could picture the stress and tension releasing as I drove. I literally visualized chunks of it detaching and flying out behind me onto the highway. With every rotation of my tires I felt better and better, and by the time I got home I felt like myself again.

While we can and certainly do just feel plain old physically tired even after doing something we enjoy (the best kind of tired!), feeling depleted by an activity or person because you simply find it/them to be energy-zapping will happen even after a good night's sleep or when ten minutes prior you felt just fine. Feeling depleted is a response to a specific situation or to thoughts about that situation.

Note: Begin to take notice of the subtle difference between a nervousness because you're about to do something new but exciting, and a heavy, yucky agitation, which usually indicates a depleting activity.

Everyone's "Energizing" and "Depleting" Lists Will Be Unique

"One man's trash is another man's treasure" applies here— what depletes one person may energize another. Your body will tell you how you feel about things—rely on nothing else. Sure, others can introduce us to new activities or apprise us of previously unknown implications of old ones (a negative impact on the environment, for example), which may change our opinions and increase or decrease our desire to engage in the activity. Apart from that, however, on an *experiential* level, no one else's preference and no scientific study or expert advice plays a part in what we prefer to engage in or not. Activities that seem abhorrent to *you* (taxidermy perhaps?) may be the precise thing your neighbor goes all out for. In my opinion, there is no right or wrong about what energizes us, as long as our preferred activities don't cause harm or impinge on anyone else's right to do *their* thing.

Note that we can certainly be influenced by individual experiences with activities, people, things or locations, and may find ourselves suddenly energized by something we previously felt depleted by (I now enjoy preparing food, for example, while it used to be a dreaded chore). However, our propensity to feel energized or depleted by something can generally be likened to the "chemistry" in a romantic relationship; we either feel it or we don't. Working as an actor on commercial shoots, for example, I observed that stylists typically liked (and were thus more skilled at) either doing hair or applying makeup. It was the rare person who enjoyed working with hair *and* makeup, even though they were usually hired to do both. Intrigued by this, I'd ask them why they preferred one over the other. Rarely could they explain their preferences with anything but, "I don't know, I just like it better." You'll find this to be true of many preferences, and even when we *think* we like something because of A, B, or C, the reason for our partiality is often as simple as we like what we like, period. In any case, for this Action it isn't important to know *why* you enjoy something, only that you do.

You may notice general patterns in your preferences, however. Some people, for instance, find repetitive tasks boring and depleting, while others find them relaxing and enjoyable—this just seems to be a function of personality type. When I worked at a school district as a speech pathologist, I noticed that therapists either tended to enjoy administering assessments, as I did (assessments are largely a problem-solving activity involving constantly changing variables), or performing therapy (a more repetitive, consistent task), which at that time, generally depleted me. Now that I've found a niche doing speech therapy in my own creative way that is in alignment with who I am, I enjoy it immensely and actually find certain activities energizing that previously depleted me. The insight here is to be open to your response to activities *in the now*, as these responses aren't forever set in stone and may change as your awareness expands. In general, however, some simply prefer to experience more stability and predictability in their work and lives in general while others are partial to variety and don't feel fulfilled without a challenge. Neither preference is inherently superior or inferior to the other.

Feeling energized occurs on a spectrum—on one end, some things will feel mildly pleasant, while others will knock your socks off. On the other end of the spectrum, one activity may register as a little boring and another will make you feel like completely shutting down. The intensity of our response indicates what to bypass and what to move toward. The knock-your-socks-off caliber stuff is the stuff we love. The things that strongly energize us are our passions; those are the areas that we will start to focus on expanding in our lives later on in Action Eight.

In short, every one of us is as unique as our fingerprints when it comes to our preferences; for reasons we don't need to question, we all experience stuff we like and other stuff we dislike. That's important, because what strongly energizes us is what we're especially suited to do.

In 2008, I attended a retreat in Italy with Barbara Sher, another one of my favorite go-get-'em self-help authors. Barbara has the following to say about the knock-your-socks-off, energizing stuff—about what we love:

**"What we love is what we are gifted at,
and there is no exception."**

Identifying what energizes us is critical in connecting with ourselves and discovering who we are. Identifying what energizes us at the "Woo-hoo—I LOVE this!" end of the spectrum is crucial to revealing what we're gifted at and where our life's work may reside. Although we may not show the outward signs of that giftedness until much later after we've practiced and acquired skills, we're gifted at that thing because we feel passion for it. While we may love to do something we never "succeed" at in a traditional sense (such as getting rich, landing our own talk show or selling out Madison Square Garden), if we're doing what we love to do, we gift ourselves and everyone around us with our true selves and with the inspiration of joy incarnate.

If you feel passion for something, you're overjoyed to spend hours and hours doing it, not because you feel you *should,* but because desire *compels* you to. When you're tuned in to it, almost nothing can drag you away from something you feel passion for. It's that kind of focus that builds incredibly cool startups, inspires an amazing singing performance, and makes the very best third-grade teachers.

Passion is where it's at. We all have it, but some of us allowed that passion to be buried. It's just waiting to be unearthed.

But don't worry about that now; we'll get to passion in Action Eight. For now, we're just going to notice what energizes or depletes us and where, approximately, the intensity of those responses falls on the spectrum between "blech" and "dancing in the streets."

But What if Everything Feels Depleting?

Okay, but what if I'm so out of touch with myself that I don't really feel energized by *anything*? What if *everything* feels depleting?? Fair enough. If that's the case, even though completing this chapter will take a bit of effort on your part, you'll really benefit from this Action—you're in need of a major recharge! Don't even *think* about skipping ahead! Remember in the last Action when you were hungry and responded by eating something? On a basic level, that felt good, right? Here, we're simply expanding on those observations about physical needs and starting to become aware of other activities that *feel good to us*.

We automatically gravitate toward what energizes us—things we dig doing, people we like to be around, places we enjoy visiting, stuff we surround ourselves with in our homes—even if we've never used that terminology or thought about it like that before. Start to observe how you vote with your feet—what are the things you notice that you're already choosing to do because you enjoy them? Like following the money in politics, observing where you invest your time and energy will provide you with vital information about yourself and your preferences.

I used to think that The Thing I loved and would do for the rest of my life would just drop out of the sky into my lap. I also assumed I'd be immediately amazing at it. I distinctly remember in high school, when our P.E. teacher rotated us through various sports and activities, I'd think, "Maybe this is it! Maybe THIS is what I'm meant to do!" But because I was focusing on the perception that I'd be GREAT at this thing immediately, rather than just noticing whether or not I enjoyed it, (which is where our love affairs with our passions always begin), I never followed up on any of the activities even though I enjoyed several of them.

The point is, to find what we love, we need to get out and try things that pique our interest—even if that interest is initially just the smallest spark. With our attention attuned to how we feel when we're engaging with people or activities, rather than on our performance or what we predict or want the result to be, we can experience the new with an open mind. Approaching activities in this way allows us to freely experiment and play, which is the space in which we will be most attuned to our feelings of being energized. Once we find something we enjoy, then we take the next step, whatever that is, to further engage with that activity. If we enjoy that step, we take another. It's actually that simple. You probably won't find the things you love sitting in your living room by yourself. You *might*, but by engaging in things you find interesting, you up your chances by about a zillion percent. When we take steps, we create pathways for what we love to enter our lives.

A suggestion: Refrain from placing any judgment on what you find you're exploring, enjoying, and spending time on. Like I said, it doesn't have to be The One Thing that we do for the rest of our lives, lead to anything huge or make us a lot of money. Focusing on the result will take you out of the present, which is the only place you will notice whether or not you are enjoying something. Putting that much pressure on one poor little activity will most likely kill the joy in it sooner or later anyway. It's like wanting to know if you'll get married after the first date! We simply cannot predict the future, so give yourself a break and get out there and have some fun. The point is to just start noticing what we enjoy.

An example: Almost every night before bed I play a word game on my phone for ten or fifteen minutes. At one time in my life I would have determined that the game was a waste of time and stopped playing. But not anymore. Everything that's there is there for a reason, although we don't have to know what that reason is. In my case, playing the game relaxes me and has become part of my bedtime routine. But primarily? I just enjoy it. It's fun! And that's important. As much as possible here, just *notice* what you enjoy without having to overlay an opinion about it.

You're probably already aware of at least one or two clear preferences and dislikes (maybe you like avocados and despise popcorn), but if you've truly lost touch with your sense of enjoyment and can't identify anything that you love, don't despair; that's why you're here!

Definitely do rule out clinical depression, but if that's not the issue you're dealing with, realize that when we engage in a lot of activities that drain us over a long period of time (working at a career that doesn't suit us, for example), we can end up feeling disconnected from ourselves, down and uninterested in life. Years of stuffing our feelings down and trudging ahead will numb not only the pain, but will also attenuate the pleasure. Here, we're going to start geo-caching—looking for increases or decreases in our energy levels.

Warning

During the process of observing your energy levels, it's possible that you may notice activities in which you've invested significant time and money are actually depleting for you. Ouch. If you begin to notice every time you enter your place of work, for example, that you experience a heavy, unpleasant feeling of disgust and feel nauseated, at some point you might want to examine whether or not you're spending your days in a place that's right for you. But don't go there yet. Just notice your energy levels at this point.

These kinds of realizations and analysis can be extremely difficult and painful, particularly if we've identified with that activity (being a teacher or an electrician, for example) and have built a sense of self worth around it. If that activity provides a significant portion of our income as well, then it's all the more difficult.

Admitting that what you've spent the last ten or twenty years doing was something you actually never liked can be a tough one. Whatever reason you chose that path back then was valid for you at the time. You've probably learned a ton and gained valuable insight and skills you'll use in your next venture in absolutely unexpected ways. What was right for us a year or ten years ago may not be right for us now. We get to grow and change, have epiphanies and go on new adventures. That's not only okay, it's terrific!

Know that if you're willing to take a look at things with honesty, realizing that there is no shame in throwing in the towel when and if it's time to do so, you can begin to honor who you are. But don't feel as if you need to or are under any obligation to make immediate changes. Sometimes all that's necessary is a shift in awareness. Change will occur naturally as your awareness expands, as you spend more time on the things you enjoy, and as you move closer and closer to who you truly are.

Like I Said...

In this Action, I want you to start playing. Remember that what we might call "serious interests" can be play too! You don't have to be blowing bubbles all day or constantly laughing uproariously andsurrounded by a group of friends (à la every beer commercial ever) to be having a good time. Researching tiger populations in India or visiting a space museum can be considered playing as well. *It's all in how you feel while you're doing it.* Pay attention to and begin identifying those feelings of being energized and depleted as they arise in your day. Why? *Because our Inner Voice communicates with us through our feelings.*

Is that surprising? Did you expect your inner wisdom to make a grander entrance? Maybe appearing in a puff of smoke, a harp-accompanied cloud-opening, or at least wisping mysteriously out of a genie's lamp? Nope! But here's some very good news: you've already gotten a fantastic basic experience of hearing that Voice in the last Action. If you've been tuning in, listening and responding, you'll begin to cozy up with Action Five right away, and your Inner Voice will only get stronger from here on out—as long as you continue to listen for and respect it.

A Note Regarding Momentum and Transitions

When I assessed children with autism as a speech pathologist, we frequently worked to decrease their difficulties with transitions. For them, moving from one activity to the next often resulted in anxiety, tantrums and tears. Though people with autism typically deal with significant challenges in this area, we can *all* experience degrees of resistance to change.

Sometimes I'll experience resistance even when thinking about doing things I absolutely *know* energize me—let's take acting, for example. Maybe I'm in the middle of writing a blog post and I get a call to go on an audition or do a commercial. My initial response will often be "Aargh, I don't want to go do that right now!" But when I arrive at the audition or job, I have so much fun! For the longest time I couldn't figure that out. Did it mean acting was depleting for me? How could that be when I enjoyed it so much when I was doing it?

I finally realized that my initial "aargh" reaction simply had to do with changing activities—transitioning—and not with what I was transitioning *to*. Now when my agent contacts me about a job, he has strict orders to ignore my initial grumpiness and skepticism and remind me that I'll enjoy it once I'm there. It just tends to be true that if I've got momentum going with whatever I'm doing in the moment (particularly with something I'm enjoying), I often don't want to stop. Someone knocking on the door with a million-dollar check would make me grouse. But if I opened the door, I sure would be glad I did!

Let me tell you, once your life is filled with activities and people you love, then you'll have a *different* issue! Enjoying lunch with a good friend the other day, for example, I realized I'd need to wrap it up so that I could get to another appointment on time. I felt reluctant to end the lunch, but excited to go to the appointment. This happens all the time for me! Almost every choice is one I enjoy, and while I don't want to stop doing one activity, the next one is just as appealing! Suddenly, finishing my lunch, I became overwhelmed with gratitude—what an amazing "issue" to have! Put simply, when I'm engaged in one activity it's sometimes difficult for me to imagine transitioning to a different one, so I might feel resistance. If you initially feel resistance to an activity that previously energized you, check in with yourself and see if you might just be experiencing this same kind of resistance to transition. The true test comes when you're *actively engaged* with that activity: is it energizing or depleting?

Connecting the Dots

The really important take-away here is that engaging with activities, things, people or places that energize us actually *reconnects us with our true selves—our Inner Voice*—while engaging with things that deplete us *disconnects us from ourselves. Aha!*

In our culture, when we talk about things that energize us we might immediately think of a vacation to the Bahamas, a massage or a retreat. Sadly, many of us tend to separate work and enjoyment and "live for the weekends." Reenergizing happens on a beach after we've worked ourselves to the bone fifty-one weeks a year, right?? Sure! And that swell idea dove-tails with the concept of working yourself to death for thirty or forty years at a job you don't like so that you can retire and finally, before you die, "do what you want to do." Hmmm…

The truth is, we can listen to ourselves, identify and then incorporate energizing activities, people, locations and things into our everyday lives so that we feel energized every day, all day long. Doesn't this sound like a much better plan than running down like a windup toy every week and finally taking two days off to recover, only to start the cycle over again the next week? Why not find out what we enjoy and *do it now*—instead of waiting until we're retired and possibly in poor health or too old to enjoy it. Many folks, after having spent a lifetime squashing down intuitions, don't know what it is they want to do when they retire. They've got some generic idea that they'll play endless golf or lie on the beach forever.

Anyone who's had the luxury of taking extended vacations will tell you that the thrill of empty time lasts only a short while, typically no more than a couple of weeks. From my own experience, I'm well aware that after the third day of lounging around (and those first three days do feel amazing!) I'll dip into a bit of a low; it's time to re-engage with activities I enjoy and get active. Like working dogs, we're designed to fulfill our purpose; it's just that many of us have forgotten that we *have* a purpose apart from paying the bills. Your purpose is being who you are and doing the stuff that strongly energizes you. When you're doing energizing work, you don't *want* to take time off! Well, at least not as often!

While we all need down-time, working at something you're passionate about doesn't feel like "work" at all, because even while you're giving it everything you've got, it's always giving back and reenergizing you. We only find our passions by connecting with ourselves, and take my word for it: passionately working on projects and at jobs and careers that energize us is kind of the cat's pajamas. I never want to do anything else, ever again. It's something to look forward to for the rest of our lives—way better than a gold watch or a Baja cruise, am I right? You can always buy a nifty watch and go on a fancy boat ride with the money you're making by adding true value to others' lives in your energizing, passionate work; people want to pay for that.

I want you to be inspired by the fact that this can happen for you in your life; you can let work that you love find you, and actually enjoy what you do! But first, we've got to start where we are and identify what feels energizing and depleting in our lives *right now*. So, go super-detective on this Action and dig in!

HERE WE GO

Materials

- Your IV Notebook
- Mini IV Notebook
- Writing utensil
- Small reminder item you can carry in your pocket or purse—bead, stone, etc.

Time

A few moments here and there during the day to jot observations in your IV Notebook or Mini IV Notebook.

Half an hour of private time for #4, below.

HOW

1. Tab off two new sections in your IV Notebook: "Energizing" and "Depleting." Starting with the exercises below, simply begin to list what feels energizing or draining to you, and to what degree. When you engage in or contemplate engaging in an activity, for example, immediately notice how strongly you feel in either direction about that activity and give it an intensity rating between one and ten: a rating of one indicates a very weak response, such as "mildly boring" or "okay." Tens are reserved for those things that feel awful or, on the other end of the spectrum, super exciting and fun—"I LOVE THIS!" If you don't run into any tens at this point, don't despair, but keep digging—dive into the *Expansion* and *Guerilla* sections and come up with some ideas that will expose you to new or old activities, places, people, and things that you might really, really enjoy.

Note: Don't discount or leave off of your list things that sound energizing but also scary. You don't have to do all of these things, but you also won't be letting fear stop you from taking action as often when you're finished with this Blueprint, so we want them on that list!

2. Each time the phone rings, if you've got caller ID, look at who's calling (if you don't have caller ID, just be aware of your response when you hear the caller's voice). Immediately notice how you feel about talking with this person. Do you feel energized or depleted? Does your body send you signals of excited, glad, and happy, neutral, or heavy, dread-y and dark? Just take note.

3. As you're checking in with yourself throughout the day to see what your body is telling you about your physical needs (again, use an alarm if you find you're not yet remembering to do this consistently on your own), start to do the same as you engage in various activities throughout the day. Do you feel energized and good or slumpy and drained as you talk with a neighbor, make dinner, pull out a golf club, or deliver a presentation? With your physical needs taken care of, you can be sure you're not getting a read on a general state of tired or hungry, for example, instead of your actual response to a particular activity. Make it a point to check in with yourself with small things: the feel of poker chips running through your fingers during game night, thinking about grocery shopping, or spending time with a coworker. Notice that some activities will evoke no response at all. Write down your observations in the appropriate sections of your IV Notebook.

4. Think about what you liked to do as a child or young adult. Did you love singing? Choreographing roller skating routines in your garage? Feeding chickens? Once or twice this week, spend half an hour or so bringing these activities to mind and remembering how you felt when you did them, if possible. If you can't come up with anything you enjoyed as a youngster, is there anyone you can ask who knew you back then? A photo album you could flip through that might jog your memory?

Note any particularly energizing or depleting activities you can recall in your IV Notebook.

5. Peruse a list of classes online or in a catalogue. This list can come from a university, local adult school or online educational program. Don't actually sign up unless you really want to; the point is simply to read class titles and descriptions and see which subject matter appeals to you. Also note which classes make you think you'd rather eat a cup of dirt than sit in on a lecture about *that* topic. Take notes if anything really interesting arises for you as a result of this exercise. Alternately or in addition, spend some time wandering through a bookstore or library and noticing your responses as you peruse book titles and topics.

6. Begin to increase the frequency with which you engage in activities on your "Energizing" list. If possible, decrease the time you spend on "Depleting" ones. If you cannot reduce or eliminate a draining activity, start to brainstorm ways in which you might diminish the time spent on such tasks in the future.

   If you find particular activities draining but recognize that they are also necessities in your life (such as grocery shopping), brainstorm ways to make them more palatable or even fun, such as going with a friend, shopping online or swapping a task with someone who actually enjoys grocery shopping (I hear those folks exist).

   If you absolutely cannot arrange to decrease the time spent on depleting items at this point, that's okay. Simply focus your attention on the task you're finding draining; become acutely aware of the present moment and of each action as you complete it. Many times we are simply resistant to the idea of the chore as a whole, and if we break it up into moment-by-moment awareness, the yuckiness dissolves in the present moment.

7. Prior to your next meditation, find a small item around your home—a bead, small stone, or coin, for example—and place it next to you. During meditation, bring to mind a place you've experienced peace or joy. For me it's a giant moss-covered

rock in a Tahoe campground I sat on during our annual vacations as a child, spending hours pretending and just feeling peaceful and good in nature. I remember the coolness of the moss, the texture and look of the rock, and how it felt to sit up there. Your place can be absolutely anywhere, and may even be somewhere you create, right now, in your imagination à la *Happy Gilmore*. Regardless, really picture it and delve into the details. Make it real. Now sit in your place and experience it. If it's on a beach, hear the sound of waves, experience the sensation of the sand beneath your feet, smell the salty air. Visualize the scene in vivid detail. Concentrate on the energizing feeling you experience for a few minutes. Pick up your small item and mentally infuse it with the energizing, good feelings of your special spot. Really focus on your item while you feel those feelings—the texture of it, its weight and appearance. Now close your hand over it and finish your meditation.

As you carry it with you for the rest of the week, feel it in your pocket or purse several times every day, allowing the energizing feelings to infiltrate your mind and body. Carry this item around with you for the next several days, and then either continue to carry it or place it in a special place where you'll see it daily.

Expansion

The next time you're in your car alone, flip back and forth between radio stations, tuning in to different kinds of music. Listen to music you would normally never pay attention to, as well as to your favorite stations. With each song, take note of your response. Do you have an immediate feeling of "Oooh, I like this!" or "Yuck!" or "What the heck??" Just notice your response and how that feels, then move on. You don't need to listen to each song in its entirety if you don't want to; just stick with it for a few moments as you check in with your responses.

Guerilla Energy

Ask others in your life what energizes and depletes them.

Listen to their responses and see how you react to their lists. Discuss how you both identify whether or not something energizes or depletes you. Then plan to visit an art gallery or other creative exhibit, either by yourself or with someone else, and simply observe the displays. With each piece, check in with your body— does the item feel energizing or depleting? Don't analyze why, just notice your internal responses and move on to the next piece. You're not really trying to *learn* anything here, per se, you're just gaining a familiarity with the feelings of "energized" and "depleted."

Alternately, you might try this activity at a farmer's market or the next time you're at the grocery store. What are your reactions to the foods on display? Simply take note of them, or if you're so inspired, come home with some literally energizing, healthy snacks!

Resources

Browse around your local bookstore or online and take a look at some of the books about happiness and joy. I encourage you to stay away from anything long and heavy and to instead look for little manuals listing happy things, just for fun. See which ones apply to you. *14,000 Things to be Happy About* by Barbara Ann Kipfer might be an excellent place to start!

Action Six

Sudden Storms: Releasing Blocks to Authenticity—Fear of the Unknown, Rejection and Regret

Action Six

Sudden Storms: Releasing Blocks to Authenticity—Fear of the Unknown, Rejection and Regret

When sudden storms hit, when lightning strikes and thunder booms all around you, will you contract in fear and run for cover, or will you pull on your rain boots, enjoy the weather and watch the storm pass in an attitude of wonder and awe?

Freely trusting our personal GPS is a critical skill to practice if we wish not only to hear what our inner guide is telling us, but also to act on it. We eased into this process in Action Four, dipping a toe into the water by listening to and taking action on relatively small and painless intuitions, such as grabbing a healthy snack as soon as we felt hungry. While responding to the Voice that informs us of physical needs may be fairly resistance free, you might have noticed a bit more internal resistance when you began increasing the frequency of activities you found energizing in Action Five.

At this point, you may be starting to really hear what's right for you in situations where you've previously ignored yourself in favor of public opinion or someone else's agenda. Perhaps upon receiving an invitation to a dinner, for example, you check in with yourself and find the idea of attending to be depleting. You want to decline the invitation, but still feel a social obligation to go—a common conundrum.

As you continue to practice noticing when activities are energizing or depleting, you'll start to experience the following: once your Inner Voice reaches a certain volume, ignoring it is no longer an automated, subconscious occurrence, and the angst and pain caused by rejecting your own wisdom becomes greater than the outer repercussions of following that guidance.

Just know that you can't go wrong here. By either accepting or declining the dinner invitation, you get to experience what that feels like and what happens, whether you've followed your Inner Voice or whether you haven't, as you now have an awareness of that Voice that you may not have previously experienced. It's a process, and every step, when we're moving toward awareness, is a teacher.

In short, however, with this process we begin to feel a strong desire to act on what feels relevant for us. This automatically initiates the process of bringing about changes in how we spend our time, simply as a result of noticing how we're feeling. Following the energy leads us in the direction of a life we love by increasing time spent on energizing activities (which are an expression of who we really are) and decreasing those activities that deplete us. As we advance toward a natural reorganization of our priorities, I guarantee you—one hundred percent—that at some point you will encounter extreme inner resistance to following your intuition and acting in new ways; this stuff is simple to understand but not always easy to put into practice. The key is to acknowledge the resistance, allow and experience it, see it for what it is, and move through it.

Let's examine the nature of this resistance and how we can work with it.

So, What Is This Resistance?

What is this resistance that rears up just as we're receiving clearer and clearer messages to be ourselves and act on energizing enterprises? Why would we want to sabotage our own authenticity? Why wouldn't we simply act on what we feel, say what's true for us, and *be* true to who we are? It's simple to say, as the witch Elphaba does in *Wicked*, "I'm through with playing by the rules of someone else's game." But sometimes it's not so easy to go through with this in our daily lives—*the* critical realm where we want to enact authenticity.

What blocks us from our authenticity is just this: fear. That may sound way too obvious, but hold on—I'll break this down so we can deal with it.

First of all, let's put this fear guy on the spot: where does fear come from, and what *is* it we truly fear?

Fear originates from and lives only within our mind's references to the past and fantasies of the future. In other words, fear only lives in our minds, and originates from the ego. The ego is a useful mechanism for navigating the physical universe, and its fear of harm and death serves a vital purpose. However, many times its trepidation or terror is misplaced and we experience fear not only in the face of actual danger but also when we're presented with anything unfamiliar or outside of our comfort zone. Often, outside of our box is precisely where we need to go. We can listen to the fear as a warning, but if we've evaluated the situation and the fear is not truly indicative of something that will actually harm us (though initially this can sometimes be tricky to determine), we can then place our attention elsewhere. When we experience fear, we can notice that the fear is there *in our mind*, realize that the fear is coming from our ego's imprints from the past and concerns about a perceived future and simply choose not to listen to it. Instead, we can place our attention on the *now*.

There is a choice: what are we going to pay attention to when it's time to act in new ways that support who we really are—the stories of the mind or what's right in front of us? When we choose to place our attention on what's right in front of us, even in the most frightening of circumstances, there are simply only situations and responses—actions to take or not to take. Realizing we can acknowledge the mind's fear and let it be there without paying attention to it frees us from the perception that the fear has power over us. We are free to act and respond instead of simply reacting reflexively. In this way, we stop allowing fear to control our lives.

This takes a lot of practice.

What Are We so Afraid Of?

What is it we truly fear? First of all, our personal fears are generally anything but unique; they're shared by almost all of us. Imagine if I sat you down in a room full of people and asked you what was holding you back from taking the steps you wanted to take to follow your intuition toward doing what you want to do in your life. Would you be amazed if, when others shared their fears, *they were identical to yours?* I've been in this room with all of these people enumerating their fears, and let me tell you, this is *exactly* what happened —mind-blowing.

Truly, there is no new fear under the sun. While some people's fears originate from specific traumatic events and we don't all experience exactly the same sense of fear about the same issues in exactly the same way, what we're *all* encountering at a basic level is the fear of loss of security, of loss of love—of *death*—in one form or another.

Why is that? Answer: because we're human, which includes experiencing this life through a physical form with an ego, as mentioned previously. Let's go a little deeper with this whole "ego" thing here. The definition of ego, per dictionary.com, reads as follows: "The part of the psychic apparatus that experiences and reacts to the outside world and thus mediates between the primitive drives of the id and the demands of the social and physical environment."

Every fear is rooted in the ego's terror of nonexistence, of death. Fear of rejection, fear of abandonment, fear of failure, fear of being called out as phony, fear of looking stupid, fear of loss of control—at the deepest level we fear loss of security and loss of love, which the ego equates with death.

The ego fears death because it cannot project a concept of existence beyond the physical. The ego is constantly looking for assurance that it will be okay, that it will continue to exist. Since, as noted, it cannot conceive of an existence beyond physical death, this is what it fears. Constantly.

The ego also ceases to exist in the present moment, which is why it resists awareness of the here and now. When we're not listening to our mind's chatter, there is no ego. The ego does not understand that *it* is not who we really are. Who we really are is the consciousness *behind* the ego that encompasses everything, *including* the ego: the Inner Voice. All our ego knows is that where there is life, there is also death; like all life forms, ours want to continue to exist. Hence, this fear of nonexistence is hardwired into us. How could it not be?

No matter what the fear, with the practices in this Blueprint, we can address and move through it. Your job: acknowledge the fear, evaluate the situation, feel the emotion, recognize fears for what they are, and move forward. Why? Because you want to feel free to move out of your comfort zone into new territories and adventures—into the life of your dreams. You want, more than anything, to freely be who you really are. Staying in your comfort zone has only gotten you, well, exactly where you are—and you *know* how that turns out! More of the same.

Who was it that dictated just how far you could roam before the bars of your jail cell stopped you? It doesn't really matter, because by believing those limitations are true, we become our own jailers. You're the only one who can free yourself and move into the realm of truly living. How can you grow into the expansiveness of your true self if you don't leave the couch or the "safety" of your routine that has become your prison?

Be brave. Pat your ego on the head, thank it for its faithful concern, and just keep taking that next step. You'll be proud of yourself, get to experience great new things, and find out who you are and what you love. You'll get to *live*.

In L. Frank Baum's book *Ozma of Oz*, Dorothy and her two unlikely companions, Bill, a yellow hen, and Tiktok, a copper man, come upon some particularly terrifying creatures: the Wheelers. The Wheelers sport wheels instead of hands and feet. They wheel swiftly at Dorothy and her friends, who are duly terrified by the Wheelers' wild shouting and aggressive approach. But as soon as the Wheelers are confronted by the quick whap of a dinner pail from Tiktok, they wheel away, "screeching with fear." They soon redouble their efforts, advancing as a group against the intrepid three, but again, to no avail. Tiktok addresses them: "You are wrong to think of yourselves as terrible and fierce . . . Your wheels make you helpless to injure anyone. For you have no fists and cannot scratch or even pull hair. Nor have you any feet to kick with. All you can do is to yell and shout, and that does not hurt anyone at all."[11] And so it is with fear.

As Pema Chödrön similarly points out in *When Things Fall Apart,* though we must allow a certain respect for it, fear tells us the following: "My weapons are that I talk fast, and get very close

---

[11] Baum, L. Frank. *Ozma of Oz.* New York: Random House, 1979.

to your face. Then you get completely unnerved, and you do whatever I say. If you don't do what I tell you, I have no power. You can listen to me, and you can have respect for me. You can even be convinced by me. But if you don't do what I say, I have no power."[12]

Knowing that fear is often only a paper tiger, we can and must acknowledge and be willing to take action in the face of fear in order to begin the practice of acting on what our Inner Voice tells us.

The Unknown: Fear of the Unfamiliar

Fear loves to warn us against doing unfamiliar things. If something is unfamiliar, our egos (the part of us that experiences fear) cannot affirm that the activity is "safe." We're all familiar with the fact that most of what we're afraid of never happens. And remember, we're talking here about following our Inner Voice, which leads us into expansion and love, not jumping off a cliff (unless what you love is cliff diving, of course) or walking across a busy street blindfolded. But if we're used to kowtowing to what others think and not saying what we feel, for example, then telling a friend "no" may feel just as scary as bungee jumping off the Empire State Building—you know you'll *probably* survive (you can see the bungee cord, after all), but what if…? If we go ahead with the action in spite of our fear and survive, however, our egos now have an "okay-we're-still-alive-I-guess-that's-an-okay-thing-to-do" experience. We will now feel more comfortable with that activity and the next time we choose to engage in that action it will be much easier. We will have expanded our comfort zone, and hence, expanded our world, which is the road to freedom.

Just remember, while it's a great warning system, fear isn't always correct in warning us to avoid taking action in new directions simply because *fear of the unknown is innate.* Yes! INNATE. Meaning, it just IS. One more time:

FEAR OF THE UNKNOWN IS INNATE. IT JUST IS.

So what does that mean for us? It means, *expect* fear! Certainly, as mentioned, evaluate all situations for the actual

---

[12] Chödrön, Pema. *When Things Fall Apart: Heart Advice for Difficult Times.* Halifax: Shambhala, 2002.

likelihood of something life-threatening or truly disabling occurring, as fear is there for a reason: to protect us. But remember that our "fight or flight" response isn't the sharpest tool in the shed when it comes to discriminating when to arise. Drooling ape hulking toward you brandishing a butcher knife? Fear. Making a three-minute toast at a friend's wedding? Fear.

See?

Expect fear. See it, feel it, acknowledge it, and if you find that fear is actually just a paper tiger—move ahead.

Know and accept that you *will* experience fear if you consider doing anything outside of your comfort zone, and don't expect it to disappear just because you know it doesn't know what it's screeching about. It will still be there, but you will have the choice to simply acknowledge it and place your attention on what's in front of you instead of the fear. With practice over time, you won't be as affected by its hollering. Fear may *feel* really powerful, so apply the practices in this Blueprint (particularly use the Acceptance Process here), give yourself as much support as possible (Action Seven to the rescue!), and just keep moving. You'll be amazed at what happens when you recognize that fear is a normal part of the process that doesn't need to stop you from doing what you know is right for you.

Frolic with Your Fear of the Unknown

When embarking on new adventures and experiencing fear as an expected part of the process, you might notice that sometimes our fears dress up in costumes that can be super-duper convincing. When we mistake these cleverly disguised fears for truth, they often attempt to attack us at the core of who we are. Remember those old limiting beliefs that tell us we're not good enough? Limiting beliefs always activate negative self-talk, and that junk is almost *certain* to surface here when we step out of our comfort zone and embark on something energizing and new. Watch out for it: that old stuff can be mean! Some people show more kindness to snails in their yards than they do to themselves in their own heads (not that snails don't deserve kindness—they most certainly do!); the trouble is we think that what we're hearing is true. It isn't. The lie of "who you really are is not good enough" is never, ever true.

But particularly in times of stress (and that can include starting something new), we tend to apply impossible, perfectionistic standards and ideals taken directly from the *Proper Etiquette for Pious Living* manual. Crotchety aunts, punitive fathers and twisted fourth-grade teachers emerge in our heads out of nowhere, mentally scolding, shaming and belittling us at the very worst times. Exhausting!

While the steps described in Action One for dissipating painful emotions (the Acceptance Process) will always be our most powerful tool for addressing limiting beliefs, I credit Christine Arylo and Amy Ahlers for introducing me to another of my now-favorite techniques for dealing with the snippy, critical and often just downright hateful old ego stuff that pipes up in our heads in times of change. See if any of these tired old classics ring a bell for you:

- Aren't you too old to be doing this??!!!
- You're a complete mess, as usual. Go back to what you know!
- Just accept that this is as good as it gets; happiness is for other people.
- What makes you think *you'll* be able to do this?
- Can't teach an old dog new tricks.
- You failed all those other times, what makes you think *this* time is any different??
- Better safe than sorry!

Christine and Amy suggest calling out these "inner mean girls" or "inner mean dudes" and giving them names and characters—such as "Perfectionista Prunella" or "Do it Right Dan." Drawing fun, artful representations of them or, at the very least, imagining in detail what these inner meanies do and say can really help identify when those voices arise to "warn" us against actions that may actually be keys to our growth.

When I went through one of Christine and Amy's programs designed to bust through fears that held me back, at their suggestion I sat down with my two biggest mental nemeses and had a respectful conversation. Angsty Ann, who continually feared

I'd end up homeless and starving, directly and repeatedly T-boned with Eff-It Frieda, who constantly screamed at me that I was wasting my life by playing it safe. When given some airtime to vocalize their fears, these two meanies calmed down and I was able to reassure them that what they feared was not actually happening. Sounds a bit goofy maybe, but that program, and in particular that conversation with myself, helped catapult me into taking action on my intuitions and going in dramatically new and exciting directions.

To be clear, the fear didn't go away, but after that conversation I stopped feeling the need to listen to it so intently, thinking it might have something valuable to say. I was able to allow it and work with it in meditation using the Acceptance Process. Typically, once we look these meanies square in the eyes we find their voices actually belong to fearful or spiteful "others" in our early lives who didn't quite understand who we were or what we needed—but now we no longer need to cower in the face of their calamitous warnings.

Freedom!

So...Let's Think About the Alternatives for a Moment

What happens if you listen to those fears every time you engage in something energizing but new? Ay-yi-yi! I think you know what happens. You don't do what your Inner Voice is telling you to do, and you never get to be your authentic self or do what you love to do and live the dreams you're finally tapping into. You just dribble around and around in a tiny, circumspect life—you stay in jail. Ask yourself: is this really what you want? Identifying those inner meanies can be an enormous, life-changing skill; when they speak up you can respond with a respectful "Thanks Anxious Art, I know you're trying to protect me but I'm okay; I've got this," and go about your business. Inner meanies (ego) will always try to keep you "safe," which is code for "doing the same stuff all the time." When you hear them you'll feel icky and small. "Good" fear feels exciting and yes, scary, but scary in an expansive way, an "Ooh, possibilities!" way. Remember your true Inner Voice will guide you in ways that make you feel alive and energized. Mean-spirited, fear-inducing messages that make you feel small, bad and shut down are merely old programming.

Rejection: Fear of Abandonment

As we touched on in Action Three, it is often most challenging to enact new behaviors with those whom we care most about. With family and significant others, we tend to revert to old patterns of behavior. But there's another reason we sometimes back down when it comes to enacting new ways of being with those closest to us: fear of rejection. There are two parts to this: the more obvious fear of being rejected *ourselves* and the less obvious but very common fear of the *other person* feeling rejected, and what that might "mean" about us.

For example, I may feel a strong sense to disengage from a friend who's bashing a mutual acquaintance. In order to do this, however, I have to confront my concerns about what my friend will think of what my actions might say about *her* and, if I cease to engage in the conversation, what she'll think of *me* as a result. Additionally, I may have my own judgments about myself that I'll have to face if I disengage. Will I feel like I'm being an unsympathetic, disloyal jerk? Will she feel judged and rejected by me? If so, will she feel angry and rejecting *toward* me? Will that mean that I'm an unkind person? Oh dear!

We must certainly make every effort to broach topics and to follow our authentic feelings and be ourselves in ways that are respectful to everyone involved. However, because everyone has hot-buttons, we may push them just by being who we are, and other people may judge us for that. More insidiously, however, we may judge *ourselves*.

Here's my message to you about *that*: It's all okay.

It's *okay*?? I know, you don't want to offend anyone, make anyone feel bad, push anyone's buttons, be rejected or thought badly of yourself. But here's the truth: you don't have control over that, beyond making sure you say and do what's right for you in the most respectful way possible. In fact, the way other people react to you when you're doing what's right *for you* is really none of your business. Make sure you ask yourself whether you're simply respectfully doing what's right for you, or whether you're also getting an ego shot of "I'm better than you" out of it (egos are famously sneaky!). Just understand that everyone is allowed to experience whatever reactions are triggered for them when you're doing what's right for you, and that's their beeswax; it doesn't really have anything to do with you. Believe me, I know—easier said than done. More on addressing our own judgments about ourselves coming right up.

Obligation and Comparison

Be careful about obligation. In my opinion, doing things out of obligation is never a good thing. I certainly don't want anyone doing anything out of obligation for me. Please, please be honest with me if you don't want to see that movie, eat that food, or go on that cruise! I'd rather know the truth and have you do what's right for you than try to please me. Don't you find, also, that when you do things out of obligation you tend to experience regret, anger or angst and whatever it is you end up doing doesn't go well anyway, because you don't want to be doing it? I do. And I most certainly only want to be doing activities with others who authentically want to engage in them too.

I'm not saying that no one will call you mean for saying "no." But is that accurate, real or important? Remember that labeling an action or person as "selfish" or "mean" is almost always just lashing out because that action wasn't what the other party wanted. This kind of labeling is just a grown-up version of a tantrum. And we're going to let THAT control us? Please.

Alternatively, in the case of judging *yourself*, the action you chose may not have been what you *perceive* the other person wanted or needed from you. Maybe it also clashed with the "nice person" image you'd really like to hang on to. Consider whether or not it's true that you actually need the approval of this person, need to meet their expectations or fulfill their wishes. Is their opinion more important, *truly* more important, than you being authentically yourself? If you answer "yes," you will continue to bargain with your own heart for the acceptance of others; too high a cost, in my opinion. But this is a process. Simply observe where you are in it and how you feel.

A note about comparisons: Judgment sometimes arises from the act of comparing ourselves to others, which is just another way to play the ego's boring old game of "I'm not good enough" or "I'm better than you." These are just two aspects of the same game. As we all know, if we're comparing, we will always find those who come out ahead and behind us. So what, exactly, is the point of comparing? Weeding out the comparing habit will take some time, but once we're able to recognize when we're starting down that road, we can then choose to place our attention on the present moment instead.

Letting the Chips Fall

The main thing here is to be willing to accept whatever happens as a result of you doing what's right for you. You're acting differently than you used to, and some people are going to have a hard time with that. Heck, YOU may have a hard time with it! In both cases, your job is to be yourself, with kindness, allowing everyone to experience whatever comes up as you act in authentic ways. Cultivating an attitude of acceptance and letting go of any expectation of outcome can be a steep learning curve, but doing so will set you free to be yourself.

Does this mean I go around saying and doing everything that comes to mind? No. It means as soon as I become aware of an intuition to act, I listen to how I'm feeling, check in to make sure it's intuition and not ego, and then take the action, being mindful of doing so in the most respectful way possible. This doesn't mean that other people won't react, throw a tantrum and lash out at me. They might. But that's none of my business, and it's not my place to try to control their experience. I am not responsible for anyone's emotions or behavior but my own.

I admit to a long history of what I call good-hearted but chronic meddling. Every once in a while, I still catch myself attempting to fix, smooth over and save others from their own pain either because their emotions make me uncomfortable or because I want to "help" them. This often comes with the cost of suppressing my own feelings and doesn't truly help the other party at all—their pain is there for a reason and the best thing for them is to experience it. The best my "helping" can do is to alleviate discomfort in the short run, which actually prevents them from feeling it and moving through it. Jumping in to try to save others is quite common, particularly in women, and masquerades as "selflessness," "being nice" and "trying to help."

Once I realized I was meddling, I couldn't believe how often I caught myself at it! Now I do my best to refrain from trying to manipulate, manage or control situations. Who am I to be the puppet-master? I don't know what's actually best for someone else and it's not my place to try to impose my vision on others. The other party gets to have their own authentic experience and I accept, acknowledge and allow that. Sometimes I'll experience my own unpleasant reaction to being myself, or to others' responses when I'm being authentic and I accept, acknowledge and allow that as well. It's not always easy. As they say, sometimes the truth hurts.

Allowing ourselves and others to experience our own emotional responses to what we do or say is really and truly a gift, although sometimes it's hard for either party to see it that way. If they experience something they might label as "negative", this is showing them where *they're* stuck in their journey of self-awareness. They may or may not see or appreciate this, and that's entirely their business. There's nothing more annoying than someone trying to teach an unwanted lesson to another; we can really only ever speak for ourselves. Observing our own reaction to *their* reaction, however, can be extremely instructive for *us*.

The choice to act on what feels right for you and to release expectations of outcome takes practice, but it will prove to you that living an authentic life can actually be done. Ask yourself this: do you really even *want* friends who will reject you for being yourself? So in a way, this might be a "separating the sheep from the goats" kind of thing for you. Staying humble and minding our own business with this process, we find that eventually, when we're true to ourselves, we're surrounded by people who "get" us and who are on board with taking responsibility for their own lives as well. It's difficult at first, but once you get the hang of this stuff, it's a game changer!

Regret: The Fear of Doing it "Wrong"

The fear of making a "wrong" decision that we'll regret: Ah, a worthy opponent.

"What if I wish I'd done something different?"
"What if I pick the wrong thing/person/job/activity?"

"What if I miss the opportunity of a lifetime?"

What if, what if, what if??

Stop.

When we're consciously expanding our awareness of what our Inner Voice tells us and acting on it, that's the best we can do. And that's great! Sometimes we will mistake ego for the Inner Voice. Give yourself a break—learning new ways of being takes practice! At times we may wish we'd done things differently in hindsight because we think we know how things would have turned out had we gone a different direction. The truth is we don't know, we'll never know, and we simply have to go with what our Inner Voice tells us at the time. What is, is. Period. It's all an experience and a process, and hoeing our own row is a heck of a lot better than listening to someone else's opinion of what we should do with our lives!

Now of course we can always pay attention, learn and incorporate others' experiences, evaluating their advice and seeing if it resonates with us. But beyond that there's the moment when we must make our own decision, and at that moment we must go with what we know is right for us, with what we feel. After that? LET IT GO. Besides, many times if we make a decision and immediately feel it's not the right one for us, we can then make a different decision—what's wrong with that?

Check in on this: do you believe, somewhere in the recesses of your mind, that someone else is standing out in front of you holding up your map for you to follow? They are not. Do you think there is one "Right Way?" There is not. Where are the Mistake Police, lights flashing, pulling you over when you've done something that next time you'll execute a little differently? Answer: they aren't there.

What's *there* is your mind, ready to play some lame, sad old recording of something your big brother said to discourage you from messing with his Legos when you were eight years old, like, "You idiot! You always mess things up!!" You were eight. Now you're not. Don't buy into it anymore. Okay, it's a *little* more complex than that, but all it requires is a willingness to allow and experience those old emotions as they arise.

Getting to where you find out what your dreams are requires

following your *own* inner guidance, period. While others' input can certainly be helpful to consider, no one can tell you what's right for you but *you*.

The Kindness Component

When we let go of the fear of regret, we give ourselves permission to freely make decisions in our lives. But there's a second part, a key component in living an authentic life: a promise. I'm encouraging you here to make a specific commitment to yourself:

No matter what, I will show myself kindness.

Promising not to beat yourself up *no matter what* allows you to move into new territory without the fear of regretting decisions, making mistakes or getting "off-track." As far as I'm concerned, we're here to learn and experience and relax into our true selves, not play it safe and spin around on that same little hamster wheel. Your ego (the part of you that wants to keep you safe, remember, by doing the same comfortable things all the time) is the only part of you that will ever "beat you up." You don't have to buy into its lousy old recriminations.

Just think, what if you accepted that sometimes you'd make what you and others might label "mistakes" and that sometimes you'd perceive that maybe a different action would have yielded "better" results? Better yet, what if there *were* no mistakes, and that everything is exactly as it is meant to be? Things are how they are because that's how they are, and if that's our definition of "meant to be," then we're always right smack-dab in the center of where we're supposed to be. What if you realized that all of your experiences are simply part of life and that you can accept them and move on?

I'll tell you what happens when you accept these things: you become braver, you learn faster, and you rapidly get in touch with and are able to act upon your Inner Voice in an intimate, consistent way. And you have a LOT more fun!

When you promise kindness to yourself no matter what, you stop wasting time on self-bashings. You stop needing extra time to heal and recover from those self-inflicted internal wounds and bruises and you get to just sit back, review what happened, and decide (if appropriate) to do things in a different way next time. You pick yourself up, dust yourself off, and get going. Or you sit there with it as long as you need to. Maybe you dive in to the Acceptance Process. Perhaps you also find some stuff from your "energizing" list to get you out of a slump that's become a habit and back into a healthy state of being. For me, the gym or some other physical exercise is invaluable for this. Seriously, who does it help when you let your ego beat you up? No one. This is easier said than done but practice will get you going in the right direction and eventually it will start to stick.

Remember: Kindness = Acceptance.

Be lovingly strict with yourself on this kindness policy, but don't be mean about it!

My Experience: An Example

When I married for the second time, it was to a wonderful man whom I loved dearly, and who loved me with all his heart, and who was inarguably and absolutely a mismatch for me. Did I know this beforehand? Yes. And I went ahead and married him anyway. I *wanted* to be married to him and I thought we could "make it work." We couldn't, and like any eighth-grader could have predicted, the issues we experienced pre-marriage simply intensified afterwards. As you can guess, I learned many, many important lessons during this union that I'll carry with me for the rest of my life. But at the time, I wasn't really in tune with my Inner Voice, or at least I wasn't *trusting* that it had wisely guided me out of that relationship countless times for the very reasons we ended the marriage. But it didn't end with our separation.

In the year that followed our divorce, I couldn't let the regret go. If only I'd tried *harder, differently, for longer.* I tortured myself endlessly. If only, if only, if only! And so we tried it again. And lo and behold, the same unworkable issues arose. Eventually I got it: my inner guidance had been spot-on and I needed to respect it. But even as I "got" that message, the regret would arise here and there, and I found myself a little fearful of new relationships, afraid I'd make another big "mistake."

What I didn't realize until later was that my only "mistake," if we want to call it that, was to continue to let my ego beat me up and traumatize me with regret. So upon the advice of my good friend Laura, who saw me through all six years of the relationship, instead of continuing to let my ego torture me with regret, I showed myself kindness by experiencing the emotions and allowing those thoughts of regret to go, no matter what. Every time a blaming, shaming or what-if thought would arise I reminded myself of my promise: *I will show kindness to myself no matter what.* And that meant no beating myself up.

But what to do with those regrets? Acceptance Process to the rescue! I eventually fully accepted my emotions about the situation and the regret dissipated on its own. And thank goodness! I know people who live their entire lives regretting one decision, and THAT is a sure path to immobility, unhappiness and shutting out the Inner Voice.

Letting that regret go by repeatedly experiencing my emotions within the Acceptance Process opened up all of the energy I'd been spending on beating myself up and allowed me to make some massive jumps into new, exciting areas of my life. Once free of that negative haranguing and shaming, I could see that it had served absolutely no good purpose; in fact, it only caused mental and emotional trauma that threatened to bleed into my future relationships and my life in general. It persisted because I'd resisted it. I'm so thankful I recognized what was going on when I did. But it wasn't easy, and it took consistent practice repeating the Acceptance Process and Kindness Component over and over and over. Eventually, it stuck, and it will stick for you, too.

IMPORTANT: While postmortem analysis of a situation is often necessary and useful, beware of self-flagellation *masquerading* as analysis. A sure sign of this wolf in sheep's clothing is when the analysis goes on and on, causing you to continue to experience pain and regret for an extended period of time. Keep a keen eye out for this—overanalyzing is a way to hold off the pain of simply experiencing the emotions, which as we know, is the only way to free yourself from their grip.

HERE WE GO

The aim of this Action is to help you gain a better understanding of the basis for some of the blocks to authenticity that may arise either prior to or following a move out of your comfort zone. Acknowledging these fears, allowing and accepting them, seeing them for what they are and then moving forward will start to allow you a sense of freedom from your own High Court, which likes to keep you in a position of sameness and perceived safety. Court is *not* in session!

Materials

- Your IV Notebook
- Mini IV Notebook
- Writing utensil

Time

Moments within your active day and during meditation.

HOW

Generally, simply start noticing when you feel resistance to going in new directions as you act on what feels energizing and right for you, based on the urgings from your Inner Voice. Employ the Acceptance Process whenever you experience resistance.

Part 1: The Unknown

1. Each day this week, venture *just a little bit* outside of your comfort zone. Do something just a little bit differently than you usually do. Maybe drive a new way to work, try a new recipe, or wear a shirt that feels a little bit outside of the box to you. Have fun with it, and see if doing old things in a new way opens you up to new experiences and expands your awareness. Designate a new section and list "New Things I Did" in your IV Notebook if you'd like.

2. If fears come up and you're physically experiencing them

(not just entertaining the *idea* of fear), use the Acceptance Process right then and there if you're able, or make a note in your Mini IV Notebook and write the fears down in your next meditation notes section. When you settle in for that sitting practice, allow the core fear to come up, if it will. Sit with it until it expands and then eventually subsides. As you've been doing, keep repeating the Acceptance Process for any fears that arise during your day, either in the moment or by writing them down in your Mini IV Notebook and working with them later in meditation.

Part 2: Rejection

1. Notice whether or not fear of rejection comes up for you in your interactions with others. If it does, in addition to the Action in Part 1 above, start to consider what it would be like for you to follow your heart and let others be responsible for theirs. No matter what you do, others will interpret your actions in a way that reflects and reinforces their own beliefs about themselves. What would it mean for you to simply allow them to do this? To stop worrying about protection for yourself and for others? Obviously you want to be respectful to others, that's a given. But that doesn't mean doing what everyone wants you to do or trying to "fix" everything. Simply observe your interactions and notice if you might be stifling your own intuitive wisdom to protect others or yourself from rejection.

2. In meditation, if you can, experience what it would feel like to be disapproved of or rejected, or for others to feel that way. After awhile you'll find that you can stand this, and finally, that it's just not your business how other people interpret what you say or do—your job is to be you. Once you begin to enact this in your life, those who respect you and understand the importance of following inner wisdom will come out of the woodwork. Those who don't may distance themselves or fall away. If this thought bothers you, go ahead and take it into your sitting practice, feel it,

and allow it. Do this whenever it comes up and see what happens for you.

Part 3: Regret

1. Write the following statement on a piece of paper: "No matter what, I will show myself kindness." Make it look pretty good, because you're going to be putting this on your wall.

2. Place the statement on your wall.

3. Repeat the statement three times, twice per day—once in the morning prior to getting out of bed and once when you climb into bed at night:

    No matter what, I will show myself kindness
    No matter what, I will show myself kindness
    No matter what, I will show myself kindness

4. During meditation or your active day, when you notice limiting beliefs popping up and cornering you with baseball bats, do the Acceptance Process right then and there. Then repeat the following three times: "No matter what, I will show myself kindness." Then go about your day. Feel the lightness.

Expansion

Try identifying and then personifying limiting beliefs that arise as caricatures, à la Christine Arylo and Amy Ahlers. You'll see their info in *Resources* and you can check out their websites for a full explanation; their descriptions are of course much more complete and powerful than the short version I summarize here.

Engage in a conversation with your "inner meanies" about how they can legitimately protect you, and when they need to back off. Make an agreement with them that you won't ignore their advice; you'll assess the situation when the fears arise and take their concerns into account before moving forward.

If you're ready to start smashing through your fears in a big way, sign up for Christine Arylo and Gabrielle Bernstein's *40-Day*

Fear Cleanse.

Guerrilla Kindness

Experiment: pick something that seems a little scary to you, just because it's new, and do it—perhaps roller blading or a free dance class. Observe the way in which your fear of the unknown surfaces. Also notice that you are able to evaluate the situation and reassure your ego that you're not in any real danger. Feel the fear, and do the activity anyway. The more practice we get with this process, the more easily we tune out the fear's yammering.

Resources

Books

Games People Play: *The Psychology of Human Relationships* is a best-selling book by psychiatrist Eric Berne. I love this book. It was first recommended to me by a high school English teacher, David Foster, who happened to be one of those teachers in my life who showed me that being yourself is the only game in town, though I didn't really understand much of what he spoke about until later. I remember reading this book in my car, praying that my infant son (sleeping in the backseat) would keep *on* sleeping so I could continue to read. I was fascinated! This book reveals the unspoken agreements we have with each other as human beings. Once these "agreements" are revealed, we understand that there are other choices, other ways to be, and that we don't need to abide by these agreements if we are willing to handle the consequences. This can actually act as a distilling process in our lives if we let it.

Again, I'll encourage you to read anything by Pema Chödrön. I personally relate deeply to her practices of dealing with fear, and while I've given you a brief introduction to her philosophy, she has much to teach and will no doubt assist in deepening your experience of authenticity within yourself and your life.

Another author I love is Bradley Trevor Greive. I first became aware of his books when I was given them as gifts; they're shortish affairs comprised of animal photos and pithy quotes: I love it!

These little gems are chock-full of wisdom and truth. My favorites are *Tomorrow* and *The Meaning of Life*. Mr. Greive also appears to lead a most fascinating life himself, which you might find out about by Googling him, if that strikes your fancy.

If your Inner Voice is drawing you toward the arts or any creative endeavor, I recommend picking up Steven Pressfield's small but mighty *The War of Art: Break Through the Blocks and Win Your Inner Creative Battles*. My friend Mary gifted me with this book and it's continued to be one of the gems I come back to year after year.

A few more of my favorites:

The Dance of Intimacy: A Woman's Guide to Courageous Acts of Change in Key Relationships by Harriet Goldhor Lerner, Ph.D. (Clearly this one is primarily for women.)
Calming the Fearful Mind: A Zen Response to Terrorism by Thich Nhat Hanh
Boundaries and Relationships: Knowing, Protecting and Enjoying the Self by Charles L. Whitfield, M.D.
The Artist's Way by Julia Cameron
How to Stop Worrying and Start Living by Dale Carnegie
Ozma of Oz by L. Frank Baum
Feel the Fear and Do It Anyway by Susan Jeffers

Online

Christine Arylo and Amy Ahlers: I highly recommend these two beautiful powerhouses!!! If my shout-out to them piqued your interest, you can take a peek at them online, order their books, join their programs, coach with them or attend their seminars. Also don't forget to check out Amy Ahlers and Gabrielle Bernstien's *40-Day Fear Cleanse* if you'd like.

Inner Mean Girl website: innermeangirl.com
40-Day Fear Cleanse: daretoliveyou.com
Amy: wakeupcallcoaching.com
Christine: chooseselflove.com
Gabrielle Bernstein: gabbyb.tv

Action Seven

Weatherproofing: Supporting a Consistent Connection with Your Inner Voice

Action Seven

Weatherproofing: Supporting a Consistent Connection with Your Inner Voice

You're enjoying stargazing. Good! Now consider a permanent location for your telescope, perhaps on a deck or patio. Steady it with supports and ensure that it is solidly mounted and protected from the weather. Then, any day of the year, you'll be able to enjoy the view.

It feels great to start a new project, and initially this Blueprint may be just that. Good! It *should* be fun and rewarding! But often, over time, "fun projects" can begin to give way to feeling like just one more boring thing on the to-do list—and these Actions are SO much more than a project or to-do list. Ultimately, the idea is to *live* this Blueprint, integrating the Actions into the fabric of your daily life so that you're continually connected with the Inner Voice. We want to keep your airwaves unjammed so that you're living from that true-self space the majority of the time.

The Majority of the Time?? Why Not ALL the Time?

Well, because we're human. I know that sounds a bit like a cop out, but it's really not; it's just the truth. No matter who we are, sometimes the ego will take over, lots of times without our awareness. We'll catch on to its shenanigans sooner or later, but as long as we're alive, we've got our ego around, and that's okay. We've also had a lifetime of forming our habits—catching ourselves in these is an ongoing practice, and there's nothing wrong with that. Coming right up, we'll cover the two parts to understanding the Inner-Voice-Life that make living it most of the time a realistic option.

When we're living from our Inner Voice, we're authentic. Authentic does not mean perfect, blameless, or clockwork consistent. Authentic = Real. Part of this book is about letting go of "shoulds" and finding out what's underneath all that programming—who the real *you* is. Whatever happens on your journey is what happens. Period. It's all okay. If your intent is to keep the connection to your inner wisdom and live your life guided by your Inner Voice, just wholeheartedly apply the Actions as consistently as you can and keep moving forward, being honest, open and kind to yourself. Whatever happens along the way is perfect, even if it's not what you prefer or you're not always "on point."

Remember: The power of the Actions is in their consistent application. Keep doing them.

There will be times when tuning in to your Inner Voice is the last thing on your mind, and may even seem a bit silly. That's okay too. You'll eventually come around and remember why you picked up this Blueprint and why hearing your Inner Voice is *the* most important action you can take for living your best life. The more you faithfully practice the Actions of this Blueprint in the beginning, the easier it will be to continue them later. I promise that if you stick with them, these Actions will become treasured friends that will always serve to bring you back into connection with yourself.

A Word About Balance

Anyone notice that the concept of "balance" gets a bad rap sometimes? It goes something like this: "*Balance?!* Balance is boring and uninspired! Be *passionate* instead!"

Right! Yes to passion! But let's not play a word game here. Of course we're going for passion and no, we don't want to get stuck in a boring old rut. What we *do* benefit from is at least a little structure. As humans, maintaining a state of homeostasis is vital for experiencing the connection to and energy for what we find enjoyable. Applying the Actions in this Blueprint and cultivating lives in which we rest, eat well and exercise helps us maintain a clear line to our Inner Voice.

Beware of careening away from implementing the Actions consistently as soon as you start to experience some joy and freedom in your life. Incorporating the Actions into our day-to-day lives encourages us to maintain an internal integrity and alignment so that we can enjoy an ongoing relationship with our Inner Voice and live continually inspired lives of health and passion—instead of merely slamming from one unmet need to the next.

When we're consistently connected with our true selves, we are guided by our intuition to effortlessly meet all of our needs. Typically, however, this takes some time and a lot of practice. When we're starting out (as we discussed in Action Two and Action Four), consciously planning to provide for our needs is beneficial. We can use our intelligence to help guide us as we're making our way towards that consistent connection.

Of course, part of living in a healthy flow sometimes includes swimming *outside* of that flow and then returning to it, like a fish gliding in and out of the current. So don't give it a second thought if it's been a week since you last meditated and you're getting a bit rough around the edges due to lack of sleep. It's okay! Just start again. Adopt the mental habit of simply allowing yourself to start over again each moment.

But what exactly CAN you do on those days where part of this Blueprint doesn't seem doable at all, let alone fun?

Give yourself leeway *and be kind to yourself.* Beating yourself up is strictly forbidden on this Blueprint (reread Action Six if needed). That includes those times when you find that you ARE beating yourself up; *please don't beat yourself up about beating yourself up!* As soon as you realize you're entertaining negative thoughts about your lack of focus on this or that, drop your attention from them and simply change what you're doing. If you find that to be impossible, sit down and use the Acceptance Process to accept your frustration. Whatever you feel is whatever you feel, and it's okay. The point is to accept what's there and experience it without judgment.

Remember, what we're going for here is living grounded by

your true self a *majority* of the time; you're integrating these Actions and leaning more and more into your Inner Voice, into the awareness of who you really are. Do what you need to do to remind yourself to stay tuned in, and know that there will be days when you find yourself getting into bed and realizing you really weren't paying attention to yourself at all the entire day. That's okay. That's how it goes. Start where you are and relax. Give yourself what you need in the moment: get a drink of water, snuggle luxuriously into your bed, maybe give yourself a little scalp massage, read a bit of a book you love and drift off to sleep knowing that tomorrow is another day.

That Said...

All of your work (and play) here is cumulative, so the more you consistently implement the Actions, the more tuned in to your Inner Voice you'll be in the shortest amount of time. It's all about practice. The more you make these Actions part of your daily routine, the deeper you'll find yourself connecting with and hearing yourself; you'll truly be your own advice line, all the time. Remember, this Blueprint not only helps you tune in to yourself and steer your life in the YOU direction—it will also result in a happier and more relaxed person in the process, improving all of your relationships with others as well (at least those "others" who support you in your journey!). Pretty motivating, no? One of the most powerful ways of keeping yourself on course? Cozying up in the fleeciest, softest, most luxurious support-blanket you can find and continuing to put one foot in front of the other, following what gives you a spark of joy and energizes you. How do you find this support? Read on.

Supports

Barbara Sher famously warns that "isolation is a dream killer." How true. Never underestimate the power of trudging on alone to dampen your spirits—or the strength and redoubled joy a little camaraderie can provide. Instead of burning yourself out, feel free to employ any of the supports listed below that appeal to you.

<u>Friends</u>: Of the people who energize you, is there anyone who's a BFF, or someone who might become one? If so, you've got it made. If you're open and honest with them, any friends or family members who support you, understand what you're doing and want the best for you will be take-no-prisoners allies in your journey back to yourself. But if you've answered "no" to the question about knowing someone you can trust and talk with honestly about your life, fear not. If you're open to it, along this path you will meet others like yourself; they'll come along sooner or later. Just keep your eyes peeled for them.

> *Be with those who help your being.*
> **Rumi**

Note: As mentioned earlier, don't be surprised if you feel resistance from some of the people in your life when you step out and start doing things differently. When we start living our best lives, it sometimes causes others to examine their *own* choices, and sometimes they don't like what they see. Through no fault of your own, just by being true to yourself, you'll either serve as a reminder to others of where they're not stepping up in their own lives, or you'll be an inspiration to them, just as others will be for you. Just keep on keeping on. This is about you finding you— nothing is more important—for you, and for those whom you love and who love you.

Spend the majority of your time with those friends who are inspired rather than threatened by your commitment to living by your own lights. It's not that the threatened others don't love you; they may just have some of their *own* work to do. They'll either do it or they won't. That's their business. Your business is to be you and to stay connected to yourself. Just doing *this* is incredibly inspiring to those ready to make similar changes in their lives. And like I said earlier, you'll find yourself meeting some of the most amazing people once you start to fly.

<u>Inspirers</u>: Inspirers, as you may have guessed, are people who inspire you. As part of this Action you'll be making a list of those who inspire you so that when you're feeling down or off-track you can go look at their picture, pick up their book, or simply think

about them for a moment. They'll remind you how great being your true self can be. They'll help you recall why you want to connect with your Inner Voice and do what you love. Inspirers may be people you know personally, people you've never met, or not people at all. They may come in the form of a beloved author, a movie star, an animal, a sunset photo, or your deceased grandmother. Stay open to finding new inspirers wherever you go.

Books: If you're a fan of reading, books are one of the easiest ways to inspire and re-inspire. Find volumes that speak to you (you might start with the ones I listed in the Resources at the end of each Action, if you'd like). Highlight, dog-ear, and scribble. These books are your companions, walking faithfully beside you on your journey. Various books will inspire you at different points along the way. It's okay if you pick up a volume and find you don't like it all that much—just put it away. What you need to hear in the moment will jump off the page and appeal to you. Don't waste your time on non-page turners—there are simply too many great books out there for that!

Multimedia: If books aren't so much your thing or if you just prefer a variety of input, go multimedia. I'm a huge TED groupie. If you've never heard of TED, check it out at ted.com. Or use YouTube. Or Google. Or Wikipedia. Take your pick! There's so much information out there just waiting for you to soak it up. For pretty much anything that energizes you, there's probably at least an article, and more likely also a blog post, website, or entire social network created just for people who like that very same thing. Make use of the Internet and follow leads like a detective; the most surprising and inspiring things sometimes show up by simply following your nose. Oh, and podcasts are great, too. There's nothing like the Internet—an endless library at your fingertips.

Music: Music can be enormously inspirational and supportive on our journeys. In an instant, some songs will bring you back into connection with yourself and remind you of who you really are. Maybe listening to an inspiring song every morning is the boost you need to start off your day on the right foot. I suggest creating a playlist of songs that make you suddenly stop in your tracks to listen. Some of my favorites are listed at the end of this section.

Local Events: Scan the newspaper or Internet for local events in your area. You never know what inspiring new topic will land on your doorstep in the form of a newsletter announcing a speaker at the library or a guided nature walk nearby. You might find unexpected inspiration and camaraderie at a playhouse, gym, street fair or other venue. Sample the wares!

Classes/Seminars: Whether it's an inexpensive Saturday class at an adult education center or a university course, classes have always been one of my favorite inspiring activities. Just perusing class descriptions from the catalogue gets me fired up. So many fun topics to explore! Not only do students benefit from a group of like-minded peers (or at least others who are immersed in the same subject matter), but the structure of a syllabus and class assignments keep the motivation going.

Reminders: Like the reminder objects we've used in previous Actions, continue to place little items around your home or on your person to remind you of practices you're likely to forget. I have a Buddha face hanging on my wall; it's the first thing I see when I wake up, and when I do I habitually think, "Ah, yes—morning meditation." I also wear a silver bracelet I bought years ago during a visit to Esalen Hot Springs that reminds me to be aware of the present moment. It's a good idea to rotate these items periodically because as we become used to seeing them as part of our environment, sooner or later we actually stop noticing them altogether.

Groups: Though joining a group won't appeal to everyone, for some, joining a meditation group or roller hockey team, for example, can be a lifeline. You can join a discussion group that's headed in the direction you're going related to being true to yourself and living by your Inner Voice, or a group that engages in activities you find energizing and fun. Joining a Meetup group for whatever floats your boat can be a great support and lots of fun— not to mention a great way to meet like-minded folks. Check out meetup.com and see if anything appeals to you. Just knowing there's a group of people out there who share your interest in whatever's energizing you feels good and encourages you to view your interest as a legitimate course to pursue.

Immerse yourself in your new worlds: If you're intrigued by the idea of tennis, for instance, but aren't yet interested in joining a club, go for it in other ways. Immerse yourself! Read about the game, research players, attend matches and talk to others who love the sport. Really get your hands dirty. Find out what you like about it and dig deeper. You may find that you appreciate a specific facet but would rather leave the rest alone. Maybe, after immersing yourself in Tennis 101, you find that what primarily energizes you is stringing rackets. Good! So now you go in *that* direction. One small step at a time.

Inspiring quotes: Sometimes it just takes a sentence or two, properly placed, to get you back into the right frame of mind, and with Facebook, Twitter, and the Internet in general, there's certainly no lack of access! A little book of inspirational quotes can be a great refresher to dip into each night before retiring or in the morning when you wake up. Or go old-school and tape sayings to your bathroom mirror or closet door. You'll find pithy quotes that will speak to you; keep them around for the times when you need a pick-me-up.

ME: Check out my website, christyharden.com, for current goings-on. I often offer supportive programs and blog about issues I experience in my own life as I continue the lifelong journey of living authentically and breaking free of self-limitations.

HERE WE GO

Materials:

- Your IV Notebook
- Writing utensil
- Optional: poster board
- Optional: picture frame and paper to go in it

Time

An initial one-hour time block.

A few moments each night, ongoing.

HOW

The following practices and activities will support you in your continued journey back to your Inner Voice. Everything counts, and the more you can infuse your life with inspiration, the better!

1. Keep your IV Notebook by your bed. Each night, just take a few moments to look at one of the pages. This will remind you of the work you're doing, and of the fun you're having. It will also serve to redirect you when you feel uninspired.

2. Section off another few pages of your IV Notebook and make a list entitled "People Who Know the Real Me." These folks may or may not be included in other areas of your notebook. The people on this list are people who know you, want what's best for you, and are jazzed to see you doing what you love, growing and changing. These are the people who can share in and enjoy the new self-directed life you're building for yourself. If no one is on that list yet, hold out. You'll find them.

3. Create another section: "Inspirers." Your list: "People Who Inspire Me." List as many people as you can think of who inspire you to connect with yourself, to be creative and to live your best life, whether you know them or not. My son, Michael Jackson and Cyndi Lauper always top my list.

4. Make *another* Notebook section entitled "Inspiring Stuff" (or again, whatever you'd like to label it). You'll continue to add items when they occur to you over the years. If you'd like to use a different little notebook or album for this section, of course do that. This is a list of sayings, ideas, lyrics, etc., that you've highlighted throughout the

Actions, or that come to you as you're making the list. Songs that inspire you, quotes from famous people, or quips from an ad that hit you just right. This may take a bit of time, but go ahead and place it all on one page (if you dare), or in one section. Then make a copy of that page or at least one page of that section and keep it with you at work, in your car, in your wallet or purse, and wherever else you can easily get at it when you might need some juice.

5. On Facebook (if you're on it) and/or Twitter, etc., subscribe to or follow anyone you find inspiring. This way, little inspiring gifts automatically arrive on a daily basis. Every little bit helps.

6. Subscribe to an inspirational email-of-the-day service. There are lots of them out there; tut.com is the one I like to use. Check this out daily and let it seep into you, considering how each day's message might speak directly to your life.

7. Make yourself that playlist!! Some of my favorite tunes follow in the Resources section.

8. Keep any of the suggested supports (CDs, books, etc.) that you've discovered during these Actions in a basket, box or drawer where you can reach them easily. Dig into this stash at least once a week. Think of it as your candy drawer.

9. Find an image on the Internet that says "I Love My Life" and use it as the wallpaper on your phone so that every time you see it you get a little burst of "Woo-hoo!" I can't quite explain it, but just writing, saying or seeing this phrase makes an enormous difference in attitude. It reminds us that we're responsible for where we are in our lives, and that gratefulness breeds good feelings and happiness.

10. For your computer(s) and other electronic devices, choose wallpaper and screen savers that inspire you and remind you of your journey.

11. The next time you need to create an Internet password, use an inspiring word or short phrase, such as "energized1," so that you're sending yourself a little pick-me-up reminder each time you log in.

When you're feeling uninspired or low, acknowledge and allow that, and then go to any of the above supports and prop yourself back up when you're ready. Don't ever feel like it's weak or you're failing if you need a little jump-start. Please! Your supports are your life raft, and none of us are in this alone!

Expansion

Cut out or print photos of people who inspire you and either put them in your IV Notebook or on a piece of card stock or poster board. You might also write their names on a unique card or piece of paper and frame it. Let these folks inspire you whenever you walk by.

Guerilla Support

Start your own Meetup group! It's easy! Either create a topic focusing on something that energizes you that you'd like to learn more about or personalize one of the practices in this book that you'd like to deepen, such as "Meditation for New Dads." I once started a Meetup group for "Literature Loving Raw Vegan Animal Freaks" when I lived in Sacramento. While we only met a few times, the group was easy to set up and I had a blast!

Resources

This time I'm merely leaving you with two books and a list of ten songs. Enjoy!

Be Yourself: Everyone Else is Taken by Evelyn Beilson. This tiny book of quotations is for absolutely everyone.
Younger by the Day: 365 Ways to Rejuvenate Your Body and Revitalize Your Spirit by Victoria Moran. This is a book of

daily ideas for rejuvenation. (Ladies, this one's just for you—sorry guys).

I listen to the following songs quite frequently to drop me smack-dab back in the middle of connection with myself. It doesn't matter if you love them too or if just seeing their titles here makes you want to plug your ears! I'm sharing this playlist simply to get you going on your own list. I keep discovering more songs that reconnect me all the time, and I'm sure you've got your own list, or soon will! Now get crackin'!

My playlist:

1. Cher: "A Different Kind of Love Song"
2. Coldplay: "Yellow"
3. Celine Dion: "That's the Way It Is"
4. Lee Ann Womack: "I Hope You Dance"
5. Cyndi Lauper: "True Colors"
6. Matisyahu: "Live Like a Warrior"
7. Christina Aguilera and Pitbull: "Feel This Moment"
8. *Wicked* soundtrack: "Defying Gravity"
9. *Rent* soundtrack: "Life Support"
10. *Chitty Chitty Bang Bang* soundtrack: "Truly Scrumptious"

Action Eight

Mapping Your Stars: Connecting with Passion and Purpose

Action Eight

Mapping Your Stars: Connecting with Passion and Purpose

You've got a clear view of the sky, the clouds have passed, your telescope is sturdily mounted, and one star after another enters your awareness. These are the pinpoints of brilliance that will illuminate your way—the things that light you up.

Now: Mapping those stars.

This last Action will solidly place you on the track to living a life you love. It's time to begin to map the stars in your sky and discover the constellations out there—to understand what the "life of your dreams" is made of and consciously set your sights in that direction.

In Action Five, *Pinpoints of Light: Attuning to Joy*, you began to tune into what increased your energy, and also to cultivate an awareness of what felt depleting. I asked you to start to compile a list of activities, people, locations and things that energized you as you became aware of them in your daily life. We then began to engage with these energizing actions with increasing frequency. Conversely, we also talked about decreasing the amount of time and effort we're putting into those items on the "depleting" list. We identified, on a scale of one to ten, how energizing or depleting those items were. Now we're going to take it all the way: we're going to identify what energizes you at a high level. These are the activities that you *love*. This is what your best life, the life of your dreams, is made of.

So how *do* we clearly identify those actions, activities, people, things and locations that are "nines" and "tens" for us on the energizing scale?

Not to ruin the magnificent surprise, but there's a secret to that, and here it is:

Engaging with the things that intensely energize you will feel exactly like being in love.

Why? Because, well, that's exactly what it is.

Love?? Isn't that a bit of an exaggeration?

Nope, not in the least. That marvelous experience of being in love—how you *feel* when you're in love—is exactly the same experience you'll have when you're engaged with the activities, places, people and things that energize you at a high level. This experience of love is the experience of being in alignment with your Inner Voice, which means hearing it, listening to and acting from its guidance—it means being really and truly YOU. The Inner Voice is not only the *voice* of love, it IS love. When we strip away the misunderstandings, the busyness, the chaos and the clutter, what we discover underneath, within ourselves, is love. We find that we're whole and complete just as we are. We experience that completeness, that wholeness, as love.

Now stick with me for a moment on this.

Einstein states, "It followed from the special theory of relativity that mass and energy are both but different manifestations of the same thing—a somewhat unfamiliar conception for the average mind."[13]

Being "manifestations of the same thing," and knowing that everything is made up of atoms, which are themselves composed of subatomic particles, which are in turn comprised of energy vibrating at particular frequencies, we conclude that everything is vibrating at a specific frequency—including you and me.

There is a well-known theory stating that specific states of

---

[13] Einstein, Albert. "Einstein Explains the Equivalence of Energy and Matter." From the soundtrack of the film, *Atomic Physics. American Institute of Physics,* 1948. Web 17 Dec 2013. http://www.aip.org/history/einstein/voice1.htm

being either raise or lower our individual vibrational frequencies.[14] Life coach Dejan Davcevski summarizes the concept this way: "Emotions alter our body and harness the frequency at which we vibrate."[15]

The energy of frustration, for example, is said to vibrate at a lower frequency than joy. The energy of love is experienced as a high frequency, and thus, when we feel love, we feel—and are— literally energized. The things that strongly energize you *are what you love*. It makes sense then, that when you're engaging with them, you *feel* love.

No matter what the theories are behind the "why," we've all experienced what it's like to feel energized and what it's like to feel depleted. We know that varying moods affect our state of being. If you feel depressed, you experience your energy as being low. Excitement produces a highly energized state.

I remember the moment I realized that what I loved doing was identical to the energizing experience of love, and actually *was* love. Driving down the highway after spending several days working on a project that very strongly energized me, I remember marveling that I was having exactly the same internal experience as when I'd been in love—with a person. *Exactly* the same! What we're energized by is what we love, which IS love, materialized. Who we are ourselves, underneath everything, is *also* love.

When we're doing what we love, we are aligned with who we truly are, which IS love.

You know how when you're in love with someone, you just want to enjoy their company and express your care and appreciation? This is the relationship we start to experience with ourselves when we commit to following what energizes us. Inexplicably, things just start falling into place. Our Inner Voice always directs us toward what energizes us—toward itself. Toward love.

---

[14] To view the Human Emotions Vibration Analysis Frequency Ranges chart, see http://www.innertranquillity.com.au/human-emotions-vibrational-frequency-ranges

[15] Davcevski, Dejan. "Best 3: Emotions, Frequency and Vibration." *LifeCode*, 10 Apr 2013. Web. 31 Dec 2013.
http://www.lifecoachcode.com/best-3-emotions-frequency-and-vibration/

I don't mean that our Inner Voice *sounds* lov*ing*. *I mean that it is love itself.*

Each decision to choose what energizes us is a freedom-seed we plant in our own garden. As we water those seeds by supporting ourselves, showing ourselves kindness, allowing calm into our lives, and doing what energizes us, the seeds sprout and flourish, and we begin to harvest the most astonishing experience of love and joy. *This* is what is actually being referred to when we hear those entreaties to "do what you love" and "live your dreams," although not many people know this. They think "doing what you love" means playing violin or writing a book. And it *does* mean that, if that's what you love, and that's where we start. But that's not the half of it. What most people don't understand is that living a life you love means, literally, *living in a state of love*.

We live in this state of love by experiencing, on deeper and deeper levels, who we really are. Doing what we love reminds us of who we'd forgotten we were. Doing what we love brings love into physical form.

Remember, that feeling of being energized *is* love, and is who we really are. It's not an easy one to grasp, but when you do— woo-hoo! Watch out: your life will never be the same again! As I've said before, making the choice to follow the energizing feelings (aligning with your true self and bringing love into physical form), is very simple, but not always easy. It is, however, quite possible to initiate and respond to your life moment by moment, choosing to be guided by your own stars every step of the way, living in that state of love. It just takes practice, which is what our lives are for.

This may very well seem pretty far out to you. Fair enough. But in truth it's not imperative that you agree with me that love is behind the feeling of being energized. The important thing is to notice what gives you energy—a lot of energy—and then *do* it.

Your take-away here is that when you experience highly energizing activities, people, places or things, you will experience feelings identical to being-in-love-feelings. Keep your heart peeled (literally, stay open) for those, and follow them.

Bring on the Magic!

We're all unique, and our preferences, as we discussed in Action Five, are all our own. What makes us different is what makes us *us,* and our individual preferences guide us toward our work and play in the world. When we align ourselves with the flow of the love we feel inside of us when we're highly energized by consistently choosing the actions, people, locations and things that inspire us, magical things happen. Serendipitous coincidences occur and doors we could never have dreamed of open for us. It absolutely cannot be logically explained, although many have tried. In his book *Synchronicity: An Acausal Connecting Principle*, Carl Jung coined the term "synchronicity," commenting that "...the connection of events may in certain circumstances be other than causal, and requires another principal of explanation." Jung quotes Avicenna's *Liber Sextus Naturalium*, ". . .when therefore the soul of a man falls into a great excess of any passion, it can be proved by experiment that it binds things and alters them in the way it wants." In other words, when we follow our hearts, magic happens. The key phrase here, however, is *follow our hearts*, not *lead with our minds*.

I will give you my word that I experience synchronicity all the time in my own life. This stuff knocks my socks off, and each time I become aware that it's happening I wink at my Inner Voice and realize how fortunate I am to live this way, and how grateful I am to be so *alive to my life.*

This moment-by-moment aliveness is who *you* are, too; you have the tools and skills now to begin creating a life that reflects your true self, which is simply how you feel when you're doing the things that highly energize you. Continue to choose what you enjoy, investing in those things that dramatically increase your energy and make you feel alive. Continue to allow those activities, individuals, thoughts and objects that do the opposite to fade away. This is a process, but over time you will notice that it becomes easier and easier to simply say "YES" to that energy of joy, to that feeling of "Oh my goodness I want to do that," and "No thanks" to everything else. Let go of how you will get there. Simply stay in the present moment. What happens is that as you begin to witness the magical results of taking these actions, you become stronger and stronger, more and more confident in your ability to trust the wisdom of your Inner Voice. Your life becomes a vivid and thriving opportunity for fully living what it means to be here, now.

Now that we've got the big picture, let's go over some last details.

How Do I Really Know My Inner Voice Is My Inner Voice?

At this point in your journey, you have a better understanding of the Actions and the Blueprint as a whole. Because of that, I'd like to delve a little deeper now into the question, "How do I know when it's really my Inner Voice and when it's not?"

The task here is to begin to discriminate between ego (which will react with versions of fear) and your true self (which will present as feelings of love in the form of inspiration, intense interest, etc.). That *sounds* simple, but sometimes in practice it won't be entirely clear. Feelings flash into our awareness within hundredths of a second, and ego can very quickly drop in over that initial feeling, leaving you confused as to which came first. In addition, the ego's fear won't always clearly identify itself as such, hiding its real motive behind false fronts such as bravado or even kindness. On top of that, the fear we experience when we're inspired toward new actions can initially be easily confused as the Inner Voice's "no-no-no" headshake. The good news is that in the end, accurately discriminating between ego and the Inner Voice simply takes practice. Over time, by observing yourself, you will begin to recognize which is which. Until then, keep an eye out for the following clues.

First of all, remember that your Inner Voice will always speak to you about possibilities, and when you feel the urging of your inner guidance you will also feel expansive and good. A moment later, when you start to *think* about the feeling (as opposed to just feeling it), you may feel anxious or scared, but that's okay.

The way it typically works is that you'll have a strong, energizing feeling about something (a.k.a., "Oh, GOODY!"), and doubt will only creep in when you start to analyze. This can occur in a millisecond; the mind is very tricky. Able only to reference past events, the mind fears anything new and anything it can view as a threat to your security. It's not uncommon, for example, to become inspired to start a new project and then begin to feel anxious and overwhelmed as you start thinking about *how* to make it happen.

When this happens, recall that we don't need to think about "how" it will happen. We simply cannot predict the future. Remember, we can only plan from what we know, and there is SO much more out there than we are aware of! Our job here is to consciously remove focus on the "how" and merely take the next step in front of us, going back to identifying and engaging with energizing activities, people, things and places. The "how" works itself out if you decide emphatically enough that you're just going to go for it, fully engaging in the energizing actions. Before you have enough experience to see that this is true, however, "how" thoughts can scare the bejeezus out of you if you're not on the lookout, and sometimes even if you are. Taking our attention off of the fears about the "how" is the meat of the challenge of following our hearts once we're in touch with the Inner Voice.

Know that while your Inner Voice may certainly guide you to act quickly at times, there is no anxious urgency about it, no contracted feelings of smallness. When it's your Inner Voice you'll simply feel, "I would love to do this." If you don't do it, that's okay. The opportunity may pass, but others will arise. Every moment is a chance to listen not to fear, but to your heart.

Your Inner Voice will guide you toward expansion. That doesn't mean its urgings won't feel scary, but if you're experiencing a pull toward something that causes you to feel smaller or closed down, something that fills you with a sense of anxious urgency, you're most likely dealing with something that your *ego* thinks you *need,* rather than what your Inner Voice would *love* to do. We all need things to survive in this physical world—food, water and shelter—and our ego (the part of us that experiences fear) is always on the lookout for anything that might threaten our security.

Know that the Inner Voice "thinks" more expansively than we do; this is where the magic happens. Your Inner Voice comes from the place in you that sees the big picture—from the expanded awareness of what is.

I find that my Inner Voice does not tend to speak to me in

actual words, booming instructions down at me like, "TURN LEFT HERE" or "YOU MUST CHOOSE THE BLUE NAIL POLISH." No. While I indeed may feel inspired to call my mother all of a sudden, the Inner Voice typically speaks in inspiration, feelings, hunches and urges.

Just prepare yourself to be okay with the fact that along the way, as you're gaining intimacy with your Inner Voice and getting to know how it sounds and feels, you're probably going to make some tough calls that won't be absolutely clear to you at the time—Inner Voice? Ego? Voice of your mother? Or...? That's okay. You'd have to make decisions in your life whether or not you were committed to following your Inner Voice anyway. Stick with acting on circumstances that you find strongly energizing and just take the next step, placing one foot in front of the other. With practice, you'll start to get better and better at discerning the Inner Voice. But even if it takes some practice reading your compass and making out the constellations for your star map, it's a heck of a lot better than trusting some magazine article for life advice! Remember too that in most situations, if you make a decision that suddenly feels wrong, you can simply make a different decision. There are no mistakes here, only opportunities to observe ourselves and expand our awareness.

You'll find, more and more often, that some "decisions" that will come your way are not really choices at all, because your heart has already chosen even before you consciously thought about them. You may not previously have even labeled these as "choices" because the path seemed so obvious from the get-go ("Of course I'll go to Disneyland with you today!"). There is simply no question of considering any other option. This is your Inner Voice. The "decision" to write this book, for example, did not present itself as an option or a choice, I was just suddenly inspired and found myself writing a book. Observing these kinds of occurrences in your life will further assist you in recognizing the Inner Voice.

If you're not getting a strong energizing boost or depleting "yuck" when considering a decision, however, an easy practice is to imagine yourself going one direction with the decision, checking in with how you feel, and then imagine going the opposite way, checking in then as well. This is the same process that happens when you purchase something you think you want, only to experience that sinking feeling in your gut immediately afterwards that indicates you actually *don't* want the item at all; return policies are a beautiful thing. When that happens, yay! You're tuning in to your internal messages. Just make sure the "uh-oh" isn't the ego coming in and grabbing your inspiration to overlay its own fears on it. But if you truly feel differently after making an initial choice, that's okay! As suggested above, just make a different decision.

NOTE: Usually I'll notice that if I feel "meh" when considering a specific activity, that if I go ahead and do the activity, I'll more often than not just have a "meh" experience. My intuition was right on!

Remember, you can't go wrong. You'll get whatever you need to get out of either choice. But mentally "trying out" these decisions can provide valuable insight into your true feelings about the issue.

One Step at a Time

Your Inner Voice supports you in all ways, and when we tune in to our inner wisdom, we're opening up to infinite support and supply. It may be a big leap from where we started out, but we already know where playing it small, tuning ourselves out and not acting on our intuition leads us: right back to where we started this journey. Open yourself up to the wisdom that is within you, and begin to map your stars to a life that will wildly exceed anything you've ever experienced.

All that said, just take one step at a time and try not to look too far ahead. This is your life and your journey; take it at your own pace. As you begin to free yourself from the habits that obscured your connection to yourself, the Inner Voice will lead you, one choice after another, to your best life. Be patient with the process. Keep in mind that timeworn but true aphorism: the point is not reaching the destination— it's the journey. This journey here is about letting go as much as it is about anything else. More about that in a minute.

But Won't All this Focusing on Myself
Make Me a Self-Absorbed Person?

No. When we're in a position to make creative, inspired choices and bring our passion and love to the world, playing small and "safe," living focused only on meeting our physical needs and just getting by is selfish and self-absorbed. Cutting yourself off from who you really are and denying the people in your life the pleasure of really knowing you, denying the world the gifts you could share by living from your true self is selfish and self-absorbed.

If you're living in a limited way, not digging deeper, not getting to know yourself and finding what you love, you're robbing yourself of truly experiencing what it means to be alive. You're also cheating the world out of the powerful contribution you could be making. Living in the here and now, tuned in to your inner wisdom and focused on the present moment allows you to be truly available and present to your life, to those around you, and to your world. By being willing to be present to who you are and by doing passionate work that brings you joy, not only do you get the advantage of experiencing love in your own life, but you infuse that love into everyone and everything you come in contact with. In addition, being brave enough to know yourself and act from your center is the most inspiring act you can ever accomplish. In doing so you give others the "permission" and strength *they're* looking for to be entirely themselves and fully alive; what a gift!

So: Listen. Feel. Trust. Experience.

Falling in Love With Our Lives

Do you ever look at people who are doing passionate work, who you perceive have "made it," and think, "Well, of course! They had all the right circumstances and skills! They just had to do the stuff they were good at!" It sounds ridiculously straightforward. The perfect circumstances and lucky breaks, one after the other, right?

Not a chance. At *every little juncture,* this person might have heard the Inner Voice say, "Yes, this is *great*, I'd love to do that!" but let fear override it and thought instead that they had to figure out the "how" of it all before moving in any direction, and so froze into inaction. But they didn't. They put one foot in front of the other, following what energized them. They didn't let fear get the better of them. Letting fear freeze us into non-action can stop us in our tracks and prevent us from knowing who we are beyond the prison bars of our self-imposed limitations. It can keep us from getting to the lives we'd love to live. Don't think that doesn't happen. Don't think people don't say "no" instead of "yes" to decisions that would lead them to lives they'd *love*, every single day, just because they're afraid. They do! The majority of us do!

But we don't *need* to. Really, the "secret" *is* so simple, though once again, not always *easy*. The path forward lies in keeping ourselves connected to our Inner Voice and following what energizes us; in doing so, we start the process of falling in love with our lives.

You've got the tools you need now. Follow the really energizing stuff, and once you make a decision, let the details work themselves out. Don't let anyone else's idea of what a "dream" looks like deter you in the least. Follow that strong energy, that first intuition of "YES," and don't think too much about it after that. Just do what your heart, your Inner Voice, urges you to do. Don't ambush your dreams right out of the gate with over-analyzing. You like what you like, and that's okay! Think of it as an experiment and find out what happens. When fears surface (and they will), reread the Actions, support yourself, respond to the blocks, let go of the need to know how things will turn out (we never *really* know anyway) and re-attune to joy. Just take it one step at a time.

Think about this: no matter *what* your life is like right now, it came about moment by moment, didn't it? That's the only way life happens. Your life is a result of every choice, every moment, every response to every opportunity, every step you took or didn't take. If I may paraphrase Eckhart Tolle, the quality of your life in the future depends on the quality of your presence *now*. Certainly we don't have control over every event we experience, but we are absolutely in charge of how we *experience those events*, and how we respond to them.

And now you're at this magical point in your life at which you not only realize that you *have* an Inner Voice, but that you have the power to allow that inner wisdom to guide your every step—if you just connect to that Voice. You *are* connecting! Keep doing that. Keep listening, keep following what strongly energizes you; this is love, this is freedom, this is being who you truly are, guided by your own stars. That's the secret!

That's Really the Secret?

But doesn't it seem crazy simple that a "dream life" is just a life made up of you being your true self? If that seems ridiculously simple, that's because it IS. But how many people are brave enough to LIVE that? Whose dream do you want to live, after all? Popular culture might have us think that a dream has to be a fantastic, orgasmic, grand event, like winning an Academy Award or a Pulitzer Prize. The accolades that arrive, if they do, come as a *result* of acting from inspiration. Rewards and awards are not the end-point or goal; they're just really cool side-effects. The truth is, your dream means being YOU in every moment—and you won't believe how incredible that feels! Finding out who you are and what you love is a journey that's yours and yours alone, and only your own Inner Voice will show you the way.

Whatever your dream life is, it all starts with knowing what makes your Inner Voice say, "Yes, please!!!" and grows from there. It's like *The Music Man* song says, "There was love all around / But I never heard it singing…"

When we're acting on energizing activities, we're feeling love, and when we feel love, the world comes alive for us; we have found *ourselves*.

Here's the thing: once you start realizing what it is that your Inner Voice goes crazy nuts for, you've got a world full of fun out there to explore. But not just superficial fun, like watching a TV show or getting your nails done. "Dreams Fun" is fun that feeds your soul and transforms you into your best self. It's magical! You'll write till three a.m. after coming home exhausted from work or step out the door in the morning with a hoe in your hand and seven hours later marvel that the sun is going down and you've gardened all day! You'll understand that doing what you love energizes you and makes you feel strong, joyful, connected and deeply fulfilled. It feels like being in love, remember, because it *is*; it *is* love. If we're continually open and willing to work with and move through the fear, we are vastly rewarded with a life woven from love.

Letting Go

Remember a few paragraphs ago when I said that this journey is about letting go as much as it is about anything else? The joy of this Blueprint is getting to know your real self. Maybe you thought what *should* make you happy was writing books, microsurgery, or firefighting, but you find out that what *really* energizes you is making jewelry, repairing air conditioning units or creating vegan bird treats. Will you be brave enough to release the old "dreams" that maybe were never yours to begin with? Maybe your mother always wanted you to be a musician or your dad drilled it into your head that you had to make a lot of money. Blarney. When you really check in with yourself and find out what's strongly energizing, it might surprise you. Piano tuning? Chili cook-offs? Skiing? What you love is all your own. As you are able, let go of everything else.

Remember that even though as individuals we tend to gravitate toward certain genres of activities that make our little hearts go pitter-patter, what you love may expand, transform and completely change over time. The particular activities we love are simply expressions of who we are, and that expression can and probably will manifest itself through a variety of forms over our lifetime. Give yourself that permission to continue to transform; don't get stuck anywhere. Keep the flow of love coursing strongly through your veins! You'll discover new interests, new facets of old interests, and interests you never knew existed. That's good. That's life. That's how it's supposed to work. Living your dreams means *being who you are, who you want to be, and living in that state of love.*

Go do that; go be who you want to be in the world; who you *are*. No one else can bring what you've got!

What You Love Most Strongly Are Your Passions

What energizes you the most, what makes you giddy or chokes you up with happy tears is a *passion*. Our real work in the world grows from the heart of our passions. You don't have to ask yourself if what energizes you is "worthwhile" or "worthy" enough to become your work. If you feel it and follow it, it just IS. Deepak Chopra, holistic health physician and all-around wise dude, says that if you have a passion, there are others out there who need what you're doing. Just keep focused on what's energizing and it will lead you home. Allow it to lead you into your very core, which is where your Blueprint for the life of your dreams is located. The world needs energized, happy people inspiring others by doing what they immensely enjoy. Why? Because those people are the *only* neurosurgeons, teachers and sand sculptors who can do their work with all of their hearts—and *that* is where amazing work comes from. We all deserve that from each other. We deserve it for ourselves.

My Own Passion

Once I started reconnecting with my Inner Self, I "remembered" that writing was what I'd always loved. It's not that I'd forgotten it, really, it's that I'd relegated it to something unimportant that I could only do in my spare time after I'd gotten home from work. If I look back, I never really stopped writing—I always kept journals, for instance—but I'd ceased to focus my attention on it and thus allowed it very little space in my life.

I remember so clearly taking my dogs for a Sunday evening walk around the local college campus several years after I'd graduated. Feeling dispirited and stuck in a job I really didn't like, I wandered absently around the empty campus and abruptly "came to" in front of the English building. I sat down on a stone bench and felt as if I was literally and very slowly being filled up with love, like sand pouring into a vase. I stared around in awe at the leaves on the ground, the brilliant green grass and trees, the old buildings, as if seeing them for the first time. I was intensely aware of the present moment. I recalled all of the years I'd spent in these classrooms, in love with the literature and philosophy I'd thirstily soaked up. I remembered a professor who'd written on one of my assignments, "Christy, come talk with me. You can do anything you want to in this field." I'd never even taken the time to respond to him, although I'd treasured that torn little piece of paper for years. So steeped in other people's opinions of what I should do, I thought of writing only as something that I loved for myself. But love left untended withers and eventually dies. Those moments on that stone bench felt like coming upon an old friend, dying on the battlefield. I'd abandoned something I loved very much, and in doing so, I'd abandoned myself.

Sitting on that bench, my eyes welled up with tears. I must've sat there for over an hour. The sun set and the air chilled. By the time I left the bench I'd realized that it was not only my *right* to do what made me happy, but my *responsibility*. Who benefited from my dragging myself to a job I didn't like? I went home, cut down to three days a week at my work and began writing. I started a blog and two books. I began reading the classic fiction again that I loved so much and immersed myself once more in the world of words, language and thought. I immediately found myself stupendously happy.

It's taken me several years since that day, step after courageous step, star after star, to get to where I am today, my constellation mapped and in full view, which is in part writing almost all day long most days. I LOVE MY LIFE! Most mornings, I wake up, look around myself and realize I get to do what I love, again, today, all day long! I've clicked in to the life I love, like the clicking of a combination, opening a safe. I'm living in that state of love; open, happy, and home.

Will I want to do this forever? Am I "home free"? We choose our lives moment by moment, and so I simply continue to choose what energizes me every day. I can't imagine not wanting to write, but I'm in touch with my Inner Voice, and if it whispers an urging to go and count turtle eggs in Costa Rica, I'll go do that! Why not!? It's not really about the writing; it's about this incredible adventure of living the experience of love—of my true self — through my actions. I'm just staying connected, listening to my Inner Voice, and having a blast. I imagine that I'll continue to experience new adventures and gain an ever-deepening understanding of this experience of what it is to be a human being, living on this planet. I've got this one amazing life, and I'm LIVING it!

You can do the same.

HERE WE GO

Materials

- IV Notebook
- Writing utensil
- A piece of card stock or poster board

Time

One hour minimum.

HOW

In this last Action, we're focusing on solidly aligning ourselves with what energizes us to a high degree. This leads us to what we love and ultimately to an experience of living in a *state* of love.

1. Sit down with your IV Notebook in a private place and give yourself half an hour or so to complete this activity. Brainstorm on paper about the topic of "love." What does love mean, at its core? Can you explore any times in your life where you felt pure love? What did that feel like? It might have been romantic love, or maybe love for a child or an animal. Spend this time getting to the heart of those feelings of ego-less, pure love.

2. Make a "Love Board" using a sturdy piece of paper, such as card stock or poster board (make it as big as you'd like). Spend some time looking at pictures in magazines, your own personal photos, or on the Internet for anything that reminds you of love. Select, cut out or print these and paste them to your board. Don't think about why each image makes you feel love—just make sure it does. Keep the board visible in your home. If you don't want others to see it, consider placing it on

the back of a door, for instance, or someplace else where only you will view it.

3.   In your next meditation, see if you can recall the experience of love. Can you re-experience the energy, joy and wonderful sense of lightness? Just sit there with it. If nothing comes up for you, don't worry, just carry on with your regular sitting session.

4.   As you're continuing to jot down activities, people, locations and things that either energize or deplete you, begin to star, highlight, circle in red or mark with a heart those that are nines or tens. Don't analyze why they rate so highly—they just do. When these nines and tens come to you, look back on your life for any connection to the current energizing activity, person or place. You will almost always find foreshadowing and signs of these highly energizing things in various incarnations from previous experiences throughout your life. My niece, for instance, recently accepted into nursing school and loving it, recalls volunteering in a local hospital when she was in high school and loving healthcare work back then, too. She can't understand why she didn't pursue it as a career earlier. Ten years later, she just remembers choosing another major and forgetting about nursing until volunteering for fun a year and a half ago.

5.   As in the last Action, see if you can spend more and more time doing the things that energize you to a high degree. They don't have to be (and probably won't be) the same things all the time. The point here is to get the feeling of following your Inner Voice and being strongly energized. It doesn't really matter what the activity is. We can't and don't want to hold on to or endlessly replay events we once enjoyed to try to recreate the past. What energizes us tomorrow may be something entirely new and different from what energized us today—running up a hill, making cookies, or brushing the dog. The idea is to experience that heightened sense of aliveness we find when we follow our Inner Voice to things we enjoy doing. Eventually, by respecting and honoring these joyous little

excursions, we start to get the hang of following our Inner Voice to what we love. Sooner or later we will be led to areas that become our passions.

6. Print and place the Star Chart (located after the Resources section at the end of this Action) somewhere where you'll see it daily to remind you to continue to implement the Actions.

7. Go out there and have the time of your life!

Expansion

If you're interested, use the magic of the Internet to dig a little deeper into quantum mechanics. Explore what that field might tell you about us, our consciousness, and our world. It's fascinating stuff!

Guerilla Energy

Something really interesting starts to happen as you begin following your Inner Voice's cues and doing what energizes you consistently: you stop feeling jealous of other people's success. How can you feel jealous when you're doing exactly what energizes *you* and makes *you* come alive? You can't! Start noticing, and even searching for, others who are doing their own thing and loving it. You might find these folks in your neighborhood. They might be old friends you've lost touch with over the years. Maybe it's a relative or someone you read about in an article. Consider how they may have gotten to where they are, and perhaps even contact them to have a chat about their journey. Once we've given ourselves permission to do what energizes us and realize that we are responsible for our choices and how we spend our time, it's amazing how others' success ceases to feel threatening and starts to become another source of inspiration as we continue on our journey of creating lives we love.

Resources

Books

Here are some books that I've found fascinating and enlightening. The last three deal with the topics of business and finances and address why and how we can incorporate ethical practices into our financial lives:

Teachings on Love by Thich Nhat Hanh
How Can I Help? by Ram Dass and Paul Gorman
The Greatest Kept Truth: An Awakening to Life's Meaning and Purpose by Amir Zoghi
Heidi Klum's Body of Knowledge by Heidi Klum with Alexandra Postman.
How to See Yourself As You Really Are by the Dalai Lama
Shambhala: The Sacred Path of the Warrior by Chögyam Trungpa
How: Why HOW We Do Anything Means Everything by Dov Seidman
Sacred Commerce: Business As a Path of Awakening by Matthew and Terces Englehart
Synchronicity: An Acausal Connecting Principle by Carl Jung, translated by R. F. C. Hull.
Wealth Warrior: The Personal Prosperity Revolution by Steve Chandler
Your Money or Your Life: Transforming Your Relationship with Money and Achieving Financial Independence by Joe Dominguez and Vicki Robin

Films

The following films (many suggested by Amir Zoghi, thank you Amir!) piqued my interest and opened up new possibilities for me:

What the Bleep Do We Know?   *Revolver*
Vanilla Sky   *The Matrix*
Fierce Grace
I Heart Huckabees
The Quantum Activist

Star Chart

Action #	Action	Result
1	Quiet sitting and emotional charge dissipation	Internal calm and space
2	Daily plan and review	External calm and space
3	Dropping focus from thought & story	Mindfulness
4	Listening to our bodies & experiencing the five senses	Physical regulation and increased awareness of our world
5	Awareness of energizing and depleting people, actions, locations and things	Tuning in and raising the joy quotient
6	Dissipating fear, allowing reactions & kindness	Moving through "fear blocks" into authenticity
7	Support immersion	Continuous inspiration
8	Identifying strong energy signals	Living our passions and dreams

Conclusion

Conclusion

What a journey we've embarked on here, and it's just the beginning of a lifelong adventure! You now have all the keys in your possession to connect with your Inner Voice and discover your true self and thus, your dreams. You've begun placing one star after another on your star chart, noticing what strongly energizes you. You're acting on your Inner Voice's messages and building trust in those signals to guide you.[16] You'll recognize that you're really and truly YOU, all the time. You're home. You're living your passions, contributing in meaningful ways, and you feel like you're in love with your life—because you are.

Sooner or later you'll become aware that, rather than any specific circumstances, the *feeling of love is all we're ever looking for.* And lucky for you, love is what you *are*—you already have it. This realization frees you up to stop looking for love "out there" and to instead place your attention on expressing the love of who you really are *through* the circumstances of your life, in everything you do. You begin releasing attachment to form. When every circumstance is simply an opportunity to express the love that is your true self, and to hold space for others to begin to remember

---

[16] And here's another little gem for you: When we're following those stars and getting glimpses of our true selves, feeling open and experiencing that rush of love, we start to realize that those feelings of openness and love are *always there* because they *are* our true selves—they are the truth of our existence. The practice is simply to continue to place our attention on that reality until we are living in awareness of it the majority of the time.

who *they* really are as well, you know that more adventures lie ahead and you look forward to them with curiosity and joy. Life sparkles with unlimited possibilities.

This is the life of your dreams!

But Wait—That Sounds too Good to Be True...

Good point. Will there be hard days? Of course. Will you sometimes question everything and wonder if you're completely nuts? Most likely. We don't sprout wings and flap around to harp music no matter how strongly we connect to our Inner Voice. But that's not the point. We're here to experience what it's like to be alive on this planet in this body, and that includes clouds and rain as well as sunshine and rainbows; it's all part of the game.

The thing is, you'll find your overall life experience changing as you begin to relax into who you truly are. Whereas previously you may have experienced internal ups and downs over just about *anything*, much of this drama will level out. You'll notice that situations you used to label as "positive" and "negative" are simply neutral events. You'll begin to recognize that you're *really living your life*, that there's an underlying joy to being present for all of it, that everything is love, and that what you're doing here is *playing*. Honor and enjoy it—every bit of it. There's nothing else.

A Few Last Words and You're on Your Way

Once again, keep this in mind:

The power of the Blueprint lies in the consistent application of the Actions.

As you well know by now, these Actions are powerful practices that will lead you back to yourself, no matter where you are, and no matter how far afield you may have wandered. Being truly yourself is your only job here on Earth—do it with gusto. Continue this work, get to know yourself more deeply every day, let go of everything but love and discover everything you can about what brings you joy. Just keep returning your focus to the here and now—again and again and again. Keep charting the stars that will guide you to authentic expression of your true self, to your personal work in the world—to your passions. And go out and live; the whole world needs you and your passion! Doing so will make you deeply joyful, because you'll be living in a state of love.

People who are in love spread that love and joy and make our world a better place. Love-filled, joyful people feel compelled to help when others are hurt or in need. They listen when you talk. They are present in the here and now for their kids. They care for animals and the world around them. They smile at strangers on the street and change people's days and lives for the better. They remind everyone they come in contact with of who *they* really are. Joyful people have something absolutely unique and amazing to give: *themselves*. They're not afraid to stand up for what's right, because they know who they are. They understand that they hold within themselves the most valuable thing in life: love. They have nothing to lose because they realize that love can never be taken away from them; they *are* that love.

Again, *YOU* are that love, and if you don't believe it now, you've got the adventure of a lifetime ahead of you as you begin to understand just how true that really is.

Here We Are: Freedom

Knowing that our true selves guide us unerringly opens us up to something wonderful: freedom. Appreciate that freedom! Each day when you wake up, take a second to stretch and let this sink in: this is *your* day, and you can choose, guided by your own stars, how you spend it, how you interpret what happens within it, and how you interact with yourself and others; *you're creating your own life experience.* Then, when circumstances are not as you'd prefer and you get a parking ticket, lose your job, a friend says something deliberately hurtful, or a beloved pet dies, be kind. Be patient; we're human, which means that along with joy, we also experience fear, exhaustion, pain, disappointment, and heartbreak. That's our experience while we're here, and it's an integral part of the journey.

Our true selves *are* guiding us, and everything that happens is, believe it or not, perfect. Don't expect your mind to be able to understand why. It cannot. If we resist and fight against circumstances, we only cause ourselves pain. Acknowledge and allow everything because it *is*. From this space you can effect real change when you are inspired to do so. Honor everything and you will come back to love. We're here such a short time, and if we stay present and connected to our Inner Voice through everything that occurs in our lives, remembering who we are and why we're here, we will remember to *live love*.

And don't forget, too, that this is so often a boatload of fun! When your Inner Voice calls to you with a big, strong "YES!" nod, wink up at your stars, and walk toward your dreams, one step at a time; just click your heels together... and go.

I wish you well with all my heart.

Book Club Notes and Suggestions

It's often much more fun to read a book like this one with a group to keep you motivated and to amp up the fun factor. Completing the Actions and discussing challenges and triumphs with your group can be amazingly inspiring. This Blueprint is ideal to experience this way, as the Actions provide their own structure and the practices lend themselves, particularly via the HOW sections, to group discussions. Go to town!

You and your group can engage with the text in a variety of formats. Perhaps the following suggestions might spark an idea for sharing this experience with others:

- Form a Meetup group at meetup.com with some local peeps.
- Meet at a different restaurant each week with a group of friends or rotate get-togethers at friends' homes.
- Initiate an email thread in which you and your book group members comment at will on whatever you're experiencing as you cover the Actions.
- Make use of conferencecall.com and set up a group of interested folks.
- Form a private Facebook group and check in regularly with your experiences.
- Skype with your friends for some face-to-face fun.
- Even a phone call, scheduled once per week with a good friend or family member who's on the same page can provide just the right amount of extra zip to keep you going.

However you experience this book, enjoy it!

Resources

Introduction

Books

Scheinfeld, Robert. *Busting Loose from the Money Game*. New Jersey: John Wiley & Sons, 2006.

Action One

Books

Chödrön, Pema. *When Things Fall Apart: Heart Advice for Difficult Times*. Halifax: Shambhala, 2002.

Mason, L. John. *Guide to Stress Reduction*. California: Ten Speed Press, 2001.

Tolle, Eckhart. *A New Earth*. New York: Penguin, 2008.

Other

Amir Zoghi: amirzoghi.com
Glenn Harrold: glennharrold.com
Steve G. Jones: stevegjones.com

<u>Action Two</u>

Books

Peck, M. Scott. *The Road Less Traveled: A New Psychology of Love, Traditional Values and Spiritual Growth.* New York: Simon & Schuster, 1978.

Siegel-Maier, Karyn. *The Naturally Clean Home: 150 Super-Easy Herbal Formulas for Green Cleaning.* Canada: Storey, 2008.

Zeer, Darrin. *Office Spa: Stress Relief for the Working Week.* San Francisco: Chronicle, 2002.

Other

Danielle LaPorte: daniellelaporte.com

<u>Action Three</u>

Books

Dass, Ram. *Remember, Be Here Now.* New York: Crown Publishing, 1971.

Katie, Byron. *Loving What Is: Four Questions That Can Change Your Life.* New York: Three Rivers Press, 2002.

Tolle, Eckhart. *The Power of Now: A Guide to Spiritual Enlightenment.* Novato: Namaste Publishing, 1999.

<u>Action Four</u>

Books

Benyus, Janine. *Biomimicry: Innovation Inspired by Nature.* New York: HarperCollins, 2002.

Clark, Jeanne L. *California Wildlife Viewing Guide.* Helena: Falcon, 1996.

Cohen, Michael J. *Reconnecting with Nature: Finding Wellness through Restoring Your Bond with the Earth.* Lakeville: Ecopress, 2007.

Paisley, Michelle. *Yoga for a Broken Heart: A Spiritual Guide to Healing from Break-up, Loss, Death or Divorce.* Forres: Findhorn, 2007.

Smith, Penelope. *Animals, Our Return to Wholeness.* Winnipeg: Pegasus, 1993.

Other

Yee, Rodney. Rodney Yee's A.M/P.M. Yoga featuring Patricia Walden. Boulder: Gaiam, 2000. DVD.

Action Five

Books

Kipfer, Barbara Ann. *14,000 Things to be Happy About.* New York: Workman, 2007.

Action Six

Books

Baum, L. Frank. *Ozma of Oz.* New York: Random House, 1979.

Berne, Eric. *Games People Play: The Psychology of Human Relationships.* New York: Penguin, 1967.

Cameron, Julia. *The Artist's Way.* New York: Penguin-Putnam, 2002.

Carnegie, Dale. *How to Stop Worrying and Start Living.* New York: Simon & Schuster, 1944.

Greive, Bradley Trevor. *The Meaning of Life.* Kansas City: Andrews McMeel, 2002.

Greive, Bradley Trevor. *Tomorrow: Adventures in an Uncertain World.* Kansas City: Andrews McMeel, 2003.

Jeffers, Susan. *Feel the Fear and Do It Anyway.* New York: Fawcett Books, 1987.

Lerner, Harriet. *The Dance of Intimacy: A Woman's Guide to Courageous Acts of Change in Key Relationships.* New York: Harper & Row, 1989.

Pressfield, Steven. *The War of Art: Break Through the Blocks and Win Your Inner Creative Battles.* New York: Black Irish, 2002.

Hanh, Thich Nhat. *Calming the Fearful Mind: A Zen Response to Terrorism.* Berkeley: Parallax Press. 2005.

Whitfield, Charles L. *Boundaries and Relationships: Knowing, Protecting and Enjoying the Self.* Deerfield Beach: Health Communications, 2010.

Other

Inner Mean Girl website: innermeangirl.com

40-Day Fear Cleanse: daretoliveyou.com

Christine Arylo: chooseselflove.com

Amy Ahlers: wakeupcallcoaching.com

Gabrielle Bernstein: gabbyb.tv

Action Seven

Beilenson, Evelyn. *Be Yourself, Everyone Else is Already Taken.* White Plains: Peter Pauper Press, 2011.

Moran, Victoria. *Younger by the Day: 365 Ways to Rejuvenate Your Body and Revitalize Your Spirit.* New York: HarperCollins, 2004.

Action Eight

Books

Chandler, Steve. *Wealth Warrior: The Personal Prosperity Revolution.* Anna Maria, FL: Maurice Bassett, 2012.

Chögyam Trungpa. *Shambhala: The Sacred Path of the Warrior.* Boston: Shambhala Publications, 1984.

Dalai Lama. *How to See Yourself as You Really Are.* Trans. Jeffrey Hopkins. New York: Atria Books, 2006.

Dominguez, Joe and Robin, Vicki. *Your Money or Your Life: Transforming Your Relationships with Money and Achieving Financial Independence.* New York: Penguin Group, 1992.

Englehart, Matthew and Terces. *Sacred Commerce*: *Business as a Path of Awakening*. Berkeley: North Atlantic Books, 2008.

Jung, C. G. *Synchronicity: An Acausal Connecting Principle*. Trans R. F. C. Hull. Princeton, NJ: Princeton UP, 1973.

Klum, Heidi, and Postman, Alexandra. *Heidi Klum's Body of Knowledge: 8 Rules of Model Behavior (to Help You Take Off on the Runway of Life)*. New York: Crown Publishers, 2004.

Dass, Ram and Gorman, Paul. *How Can I Help? Stories and Reflections on Service*. New York: Alfred A. Knopf, 1985.

Seidman, Dov. *How: Why HOW We Do Anything Means Everything*. Hoboken: John Wiley and Sons, 2007.

Hanh, Thich Nhat. *Teachings on Love*. Berkeley: Parallax Press, 1998.

Zoghi, Amir. *The Greatest Kept Truth: An Awakening to Life's Meaning and Purpose*. Australia: Be Free Events, 2008.

Films

Fierce Grace. Dir. Mickey Lemle. Zeitgeist Video, 2001.

I Heart Huckabees. Dir. David O. Russell. Fox Searchlight Pictures, 2004.

The Matrix. Dir. Andy Wachowski and Lana Wachowski. Warner Brothers, 1999.

The Quantum Activist. Dir. Renee Slade and Ri Stewart. Intention Media, 2009.

Revolver. Dir. Guy Ritchie. Sony Pictures, 2005.

Vanilla Sky. Dir. Cameron Crowe. Paramount Pictures, 2001.

What the Bleep Do We Know? Dir. William Arntz, Betsy Chasse, and Mark Vicente. Comart Films, 2004.

About the Author

Christy Harden is a writer, speech pathologist, commercial actor and goofball extraordinaire. Christy holds master's degrees in Speech Pathology and English, as well as a bachelor's degree in Environmental Studies. She loves animals, nature and all things health. She has published short stories and poetry; this is her first full-length book. When not otherwise occupied, she and her two faithful pups explore Los Angeles and beyond with the enthusiasm of preschoolers at recess and can be spotted cavorting in any number of places. To find them, just follow the laughter.

www.ChristyHarden.com

Made in the USA
San Bernardino, CA
26 February 2015